Letters to a Teacher

Also by Sam Pickering

SAM

PICKERING

Letters to a Teacher

Grove Press
New York

Published simultaneously in Canada
Printed in the United States of America

FIRST GROVE PRESS EDITION

Library of Congress Cataloging-in-Publication Data

Pickering, Samuel F., 1941–
    Letters to a teacher / Sam Pickering.—1st ed.
      p. cm.
    ISBN 0-8021-4227-3 (pbk.)
    1. Teachers—Anecdotes.   2. Teaching—Anecdotes.   I. Title.

  LB1775.P56 2004
  371.1—dc22   2004057077

Grove Press
an imprint of Grove/Atlantic, Inc.
841 Broadway
New York, NY 10003

05 06 07 08 09   10 9 8 7 6 5 4 3 2 1

For Vicki, who has endured twenty-five years of kitchen lectures and who hopes this book will sell well enough so she can spend a week or two sitting on white sands, a palm tree swaying overhead, coconut milk beading over the lip of a glass in her hand, all classes, refrigerators, stoves, and children far away across the deep blue sea.

Contents

Author's Note

For almost thirty years I have written essays describing my life and wanderings. Teaching has been a great part of that life, though certainly not all of it. As a result some of the material in this book first appeared in slightly different form in collections of my essays published by several presses, including the University Press of New England, the University of Georgia Press, the University of Iowa Press, the University of Missouri Press, the University Press of Florida, Ohio University Press, the University of Tennessee Press, and the University of Michigan Press. I am proud of the volumes of essays, a list of which appears in the front of this book.

Letters to a Teacher

Introduction

DEAR TEACHER,

Before you read this book, you should know something about me. I was born in Nashville, Tennessee, in 1941. Five years later Mother dropped me at Mrs. Little's kindergarten. I played tag and the tambourine and kissed Mary McClintock and had such a hoot I've been in school ever since, fifty-eight green years. After kindergarten I attended public school for eight years, then Montgomery Bell Academy, a small country day school, for four years. Following high school I spent a year at Vanderbilt University after which I transferred to Sewanee, a place I grew to love. After graduating from Sewanee I spent two years at Cambridge University in Britain. I then returned home and taught English at MBA for a year, my classes furnishing Tommy Schulman with some of the memories he used in writing *Dead Poets Society*. The next fall I lit out for Princeton, getting a Ph.D. in English four years later. For eight years I taught at Dartmouth. In 1978 Dartmouth kicked me out but not too far. I landed at the University of Connecticut, where I have been wondrously happy ever since.

Over the years I have written seventeen books, fourteen of them collections of personal essays describing my doings. I'm not sure why I started writing. Sometimes I tell folks that I walked out of class one day after holding forth about the meaning of human existence and realized I couldn't identify the trees in my backyard. "What a fraud, I was," I say. And so I learned to identify trees, grasses, and animal droppings, these last by smell and taste, or so I declare when conversation needs a little fertilizer. Gardens bloom in my essays, so many that a friend said, "Sam, there are more flowers in your books than mouse turds in a meal barrel." On other occasions I explain differently my beginning to write. I simply say, "What can a middle-aged man do with his days?" Making money has never interested me. I lack the grit to devote myself wholeheartedly to inflating a bank account. Instead of bucking me up, the labor would depress me.

Moreover I didn't want to become a man-about-town, knowledgeable about bad wine and good sin. Although splashing about in the high octane might have been fun, it probably would have killed me and, more importantly, brought heartache to people I love. Writing is much safer; at least my sort of writing is safer. When doings in the big world hang heavy as iron, I describe the fictional cavortings of a loony bin of country characters in Smith County, Tennessee. I laugh, and streaks of gold and silver turn sunsets into dawns.

A decade ago a reviewer said my books revealed "a restless, cantankerous personality in love with ordinary family life." "That's probably accurate," I told my wife, Vicki, "except I'm not cantankerous. What kind of SOB would write that?" Still, I am restless. In part restlessness made me an English teacher. Unlike mathematicians who begin playing with numbers as soon as they are conceived, muttering "2, 4, 8, 16, 32" when their eggs divide, English teachers stumble into the classroom. Because I am restless, I have occasionally wandered over the hills and far away, before the children were born, teaching for a year in both Syria and Jordan and spending another year as a visiting faculty member at University College London, where I ran a foreign study program. Twice since 1990 I have hauled my family off to Western Australia. Travel can narrow just as easily as it can broaden, dissatisfy as well as satisfy. For me travel has been gloriously satisfying. In any case this book reflects my wanderings, most of which, in truth, have been on the page or in Storrs, Connecticut.

For six years I served on the local school board. One year Democrats in town telephoned and asked me to run for the board as a Republican. On my saying I was not a Republican, the Democrats instructed me to go to the town hall and register as a Republican, adding that they would get the Republicans to nominate me. In a gully between books, always a dangerous place to be, I registered and, as might be expected, was elected to the board. I served only a single term. I believe in the Jeffersonian ideal of the citizen steward; the more people who serve their community the stronger that community will be. At the end of six years I resisted the temptation to run again. In fact I have resisted many temptations. I enjoy teaching and ordinary life, and when opportunities of the sort the big world thinks important knocked at my front door, I hightailed it out the back, headed for the classroom. At the end of my term on the board, Republicans asked me to run for Congress. I declined, as I declined invitations to stand for college presidencies. The result has been a marvelous life in which I have remained free to follow whim and the vagaries of my thought instead of shaping word, deed, and life to suit convention or someone else's expectations.

Because of my books and Tommy Schulman's movie, people have invited me to lecture. I have spoken some three hundred to four hundred times. Most of the talks have been free and for charity. I have raised money for libraries, nature trusts, and university presses. I have tried to cheer the ill and the morose. I have also been a visiting scholar at colleges and made commencement addresses. Once I spent a week at Stanford as a guest of the medical school. Another time I lectured on a cruise ship. To buy the front bumper of a Plymouth, gutters for the house, and a new refrigerator I have talked for money. For college tuition I have made motivational speeches for corporations, their contents wallet-stuffing flimflam. At present, I have three children in college, their fees amounting to 223 percent of my take-home pay, something, alas, that has forced me back into the top-hat and snake-oil business.

Although words are almost always inadequate to deep thought, at least sincere words, they are the best things we have for communication. Often, for example, I want to tell Vicki how much life with her has meant to me. But cramming emotion and the experiences of twenty-five years into sentences is impossible, and so I pat her on the shoulder and simply ask what's for dessert—

maybe homemade pumpkin bread or better yet a chocolate cake. Similarly, trying to distill a lifetime of classrooms into 242 pages is impossible. Still, like the numbskull son in the fairy tale "The Princess on the Glass Hill," I'm going to try. In the fairy tale, because the hero is uneducated he attempts what is impossible. He attempts something rational people know cannot be done and as a result they don't try to do it: ride a horse up a glass hill. Because lessons have not made him cautious and reduced him to common sense, the hero mounts his horse and does the impossible: rides up the hill to win the hand of a princess. In this book I mount a stable of hobbyhorses. Often I stumble, but occasionally I hope an idea will canter to the edge of a glass hill, and that you'll find yourself seizing reins and saddle horn and galloping forward, if not upward.

Miss Dotty Brice lived in Carthage. The daughter of Shubael Brice, who owned the hardware store, Miss Dotty never married. An only child, she lived at home and nursed her parents to the grave. Shubael was not a good businessman, and after his death when the store was sold and debts paid, Miss Dotty was left with little. Over the years her little shrank to nothing; yet she never went without. Relatives mended her roof and neighbors brought her bacon and eggs, firewood and coal. Several nights a week at dinnertime, Miss Dotty put on her best clothes and started uptown. Townspeople watched for her, and before she walked far someone invited her in for dinner. "Don't you look nice, Miss Dotty," a neighbor would say. "We are just sitting down to eat. We are not having anything fancy, but we'd be pleased if you'd join us." I don't serve anything fancy in this book, no Oysters à la Bazeine, no Pâté Fin, just kitchen fare—commonsensical corn and butter beans, kale, tomatoes, fried chicken, and for dessert rice pudding lumpy with raisins. Still, I'd be pleased if you'd join me.

Read slowly and mull. An idea or two may bubble into indigestion. But if you pause, the bile will subside. Don't bolt the book in a single sitting. Imitate the turtle who took a hundred years to climb from one step to another. Unfortunately, on the first day of the one hundred and first year, the turtle stumbled and, flipping over, rolled back down the step. "Damn it to hell," he said, after righting himself and shaking the dust off his shell. "Grandma was right. Haste makes waste." If learning from a reptile, even a wondrous yellow and black box turtle, strikes you as demeaning, if not absurd, think of my letters as periods in a school day. While some may be dull, others will be stirring, at least occasionally. In a letter or two you might find so many ideas with which you disagree that you may imagine yourself Hall Monitor, clots of words bouncing past noisy as children, sometimes making you smile, other times irritating you, always making you long for the teachers' lounge and the quiet of coffee and a doughnut.

Read with a pencil. Margins are wide. Jot down things that pop into mind. Good teachers are opinionated. Bay like a hound and tree my stupidities. At best you will sketch ideas, maybe even plan a class. Many years ago an elderly colleague decided to give away his library before he died. "Take any books you want," he told me. "I have annotated all of them." Indeed, he had. Instead of detailing agreement or disagreement and taking argument to task, he commented on authors, writing things like, "What a fool," "The Bastard," and "She'll burn in Hell for this rubbish." Although my colleague had not met the authors of the books in his library, he described their physical attributes or lack thereof in scatological detail. If you follow my colleague's lead and write such things in this book, don't take the book to school. Yet if you must cart it to school in order to share your wit with a friend, place the book on the top shelf of your bookcase, preferably behind your collection of guides to wildflowers, birds, salamanders, and lichens.

I realize some of you will not mark the book. The educational landscape that I have wandered may differ more from yours than Mars does from Earth. Many of your students may live in dysfunctional homes in dysfunctional neighborhoods. How you cope with the sorrow and the ugliness you see every day and how you help your students are extraordinarily important. But for me to advise you would be arrogant. As the old saying declares, "The brotherhood of man is nice, but bread costs money." Hope, though, helps people keep going and doing, and I hope you will find a word or two of mine, a suggestion, useful and encouraging. At the least maybe the book will divert you and make you smile for a moment.

Lastly, I begin each letter with "Dear Teacher." I know the salutation is affected. But years of shaping sentences for class and page have made me slightly affected. Some time ago I went to a dude ranch in Wyoming. The West was new to me, and I wanted to learn to see. Often I sat on the wranglers' bench and asked questions. Horse manure seemed wholesome, and I smelled hunks hoping my nose could ferret out apt, descriptive words. "I don't know how to describe the fragrance of this," I said one afternoon as I sat on the bench turning over a lump of manure in my left hand. "Why don't you . . ." a wrangler on my right began, then paused before starting again and saying, "Why don't you just say it smells like shit?" A little affectation is not always a bad thing. Moreover I prefer "Dear Teacher" to e-mail salutations used by students new to my classroom: "hi," or, if the student is attempting to be formal, "hi, prof," the *H* never capitalized, a barbarism that makes me twitch, sending my hand quivering over the delete key.

Letter One: The Teacher's Life

DEAR TEACHER,

The heartache of being human is that often when we act self-lessly and with good intentions we bruise others. For teachers surrounded by children who at times seem sadly vulnerable the heartache rarely ends. No matter how well intentioned teachers are, they will bump those about them. Two things enable teachers to cope. The first is simply forgetfulness. Life pushes so much at us that a specific event rarely clogs the mind for a long time. In Kenneth Grahame's *The Wind in the Willows,* Mole and Ratty search for Portly, a lost baby otter. They rescue Portly, finding him sleeping between the hooves of Pan, the deity of the natural world. Before he vanishes, Pan bestows the gift of forgetfulness upon Mole and Rat, "lest," Grahame writes, "the awful remembrance should remain and grow, and overshadow mirth and pleasure, and the great haunting memory should spoil all the after-lives of little animals helped out of difficulties, in order that they should be happy and light-hearted as before."

Forgetfulness is a great boon. The person forever conscious of the presence of a god can never relax and be spontaneous, cannot embody the spontaneity of consciousness that the nineteenth-century critic Matthew Arnold said brought sweetness and light into our lives, and, indeed, into the lives of others. If the mistakes of the past were always present, no teacher could act. If I recalled all the regrettable things I've done as soon as I woke up in the morning, I wouldn't be able to get out of bed, much less go to class. Indeed if side dishes heaped with all the tiffs of the past accompanied meals to the dinner table, marriages would not endure to dessert.

The pleasures of forgetfulness often brighten small moments. Many years ago outside an apartment in Nashville, my father and I met Norvell Skipworth and his wife unloading their car. The Skipworths had returned from a vacation in Georgia. Neither Norvell nor his wife was young, and after handing the key to the trunk of the car to his wife, Norvell turned and seeing Father said, "Sam, good morning. This is a surprise, and how was your trip?" Norvell then paused and looked puzzled for a moment before shaking his head in mild exasperation and adding, "Aw shucks, I got that wrong. I went on the trip."

The other matter that helps teachers bounce into class is that the real effects of teaching remain mysterious, something that complicates attempts to define good teaching. Almost never do teachers know exactly how their words, or actions, affect students. Moreover, if we really believed that everything we said shaped students, we would be too terrified to speak. Still, the ways of words and interpretations of words sometimes startle us. "Six years have passed since I was in your class," a girl once wrote me from Torrington, "and I want to tell you that you handled me the right way. I did not think so then, but now that I am older and have thought about it for a long time I realize you were correct. Thank you for doing me such a service." I did not recall the girl until I looked in my grade book. She was one of fifty-four students and received a B in the course. She wrote three B+ papers, then a B, and finally a C paper. She made 86 on the final examination. In class she was silent, a faceless gray student who never talked. Indeed the semester passed without my speaking to her except when I returned papers. From my perspective the handling that I accomplished so memorably did not occur. From her point of view, an offhand remark of mine must have seemed directed at her and provoked thought that rolled through years.

Recently I taught a course on the short story. A tough-looking boy sat in the back row in the right-hand corner of the room. The boy always wore a blue baseball cap with an orange bill. Printed across the front of the cap was "Danbury." Instead of removing the cap when class began, the boy pushed it around so that the bill pointed behind him, toward the wall. Then he leaned forward on his elbows and glared at me for fifty minutes, his expression never changing, scorn furrowing his brow. A month after the semester ended, he came to my office. He wore the same cap. In his hand he carried an empty tin can, the top of which had been sliced off. "Hope you don't mind," the boy said, sitting down and then raising the can to his mouth and spitting, "I chew." "I came to tell you," he continued, "that your course was the best I had in this university. Funniest damn course in the world. Thought I would bust a gut laughing. Told all my friends to take it. I won't forget you," the boy said, abruptly standing and shifting the can into his left hand in order to shake hands. "I won't forget you either," I said.

To know the effects of a class upon students or rather how students think a class affects them would be disturbing. Thirty years ago at Dartmouth if I had known how my class affected Gail, my children would not be named Francis, Edward, and Eliza. I was young and unmarried. All I remember about Gail is that she had brown hair, sat in the first row, once wore a yellow dress, and that I was in love with her. I was so in love I could not bear to look at her, much less speak to her. When she missed class, the room seemed empty. At the end of the semester Gail vanished. At a reunion five years later, George, another student from that class, visited me. "Sam," he said, as we sat in my living room, "do you remember a girl in your class named Gail? She sat in the front row and had brown hair." "Yes, slightly," I said, feeling uncomfortable. "Goodness," George exclaimed, "was she in love with you! The whole class knew it. Some days she couldn't face you and wouldn't attend. Isn't that the darnedest thing?" "Yes, George," I said, "the darnedest thing."

If not the place for mongrel love, the classroom is a place for unrequited liking. More important even than knowing a subject well is the capacity for liking students. Of course exceptions exist to this and to all I write. The person teaching medical school must insure that students know the difference between heart and colon. Otherwise his pupils will perform extraordinary bypasses. Although I think personality combined with knowledge is essential in a teacher, to a great degree we teachers don't matter.

In comparison to students we exist to be outgrown and forgotten, alas, like parents. On sunny days I explore graveyards. Engraved on a tombstone I saw in Missouri was a tribute praising a man for achieving "sweet oblivion of self," a state almost never achieved but perhaps one to be wished for. Although the teacher's "self" affects classrooms, students matter more than we do.

I have aged into buying used books. Clean, pressed pages appear uninformed and smack of naïveté and its sometime companion cruelty. Nowadays I prefer books worn and watermarked, tattered like me, their margins beaten into seams, their words seemingly bruised into wisdom by handling. Because I hope to find wisdom, I usually find it. Recently I bought *In Nature's Realm,* published in 1900 and written by Charles Conrad Abbott, a once popular but now obscure naturalist and scientist. "Ascribe infallibility to the professor," Abbott wrote, "and you become at best his echo, and condemn to slavery what should be free as the air, your own mind." Abbott's remark applies more to college and graduate students than it does to children in elementary and high school. Yet his point matters. When you and I enable children to grow beyond us and shape thoughts different from our own, we have done well.

We should take short views of life and try to help children through the present. We are not shaping, as commencement speakers tediously phrase it, "the future of America." We are helping children. Do not look so far into the future that you lose the moment. To be sure, we frequently teach skills children will use, but more often than not we just help. At our best we broaden the possibilities of their lives. In "Tintern Abbey," the English poet William Wordsworth described what he called "that best portion of a good man's life / His little, nameless, unremembered acts / Of kindness and of love." Often what children will remember from your classroom are little decencies, things you forgot as soon as you did them, things you did out of love, not out of love for an individual but out of the love that blossoms from an appreciation of this great gift called life. "When I began first grade," a girl in one of my classes told me, "I was homesick. Every morning I had funny feelings and went to the nurse's office, and she called Mom." After the first week of school the principal talked to the girl's mother. He suggested the mother pack an affectionate note into her daughter's lunch box every day. "When I opened my lunch box and saw the notes, I was so happy," the girl said. The funny feelings vanished, but the notes and the principal's concern continued. Throughout the year when he saw her in the hall, the principal asked the girl if she had received a note that day. "I won't forget him," my student told me. "He was so kind, and that's important."

Influence

Sometimes, alas, your classroom will provide structure for children's lives, structures children do not have at home, if they have homes. In general, however, our influence is more limited or is limited to lessons we often do not know we are teaching. Occasionally, though, I delude myself into thinking that I am

Delphic or, as sloganeers put it, I am making a difference. Happily classrooms provide antidotes to delusions of influence.

Two years ago I taught the short story to a small class. Enrolled in the course were two members of the girls' basketball team, one of the girls the best player in the nation. When the team won the national championship, I told friends that my inspirational teaching had so influenced the girls that, as athletic cognoscenti phrase it, they raised their game to a new level. If the girls had not taken my course, the team would have lost more games than it won, or so I said until the final examination. At the examination students wrote their names and the names of their teachers on the fronts of blue books. The best player in the nation knew her name. Alas, she thought me Mr. Peckerington. "Perhaps," Vicki said at dinner, "your teaching did not determine the outcome of the game against Tennessee." "Maybe, maybe not," I said. "Influence is difficult to determine." You will, of course, have many names. Relish escaping mundane identity and enjoy being someone else. Mrs. Underwood will be Mrs. Underwear. Every year I teach a course on American nature writers. One day when I walked into class, I noticed the notebook of my best student. Scrawled across the top of the notebook was "Nature Writing—Mr. Pickmenose."

Even when the going seems good to you, it may not strike students that way. This past fall I taught a course in the personal essay. I thought the first day of class went wonderfully. I knew I had performed stunningly. "How was it?" Vicki said that night. "Luminous," I said. "I was a beacon of light." The next day I went to the university bookstore and chatted with my friend Suzy. "One of your students wandered into my office yesterday," she said. The boy was lost and did not know where to find books for his course. "I'm looking for a book called *The Art of the Personal Essay*," he said. "What's the name of the course?" Suzy asked. "I don't know," the boy said. "What's the teacher's name?" Suzy then asked. "Pick-something," the boy said. "Pickering?" Suzy asked. "Yes, that's the name," the boy said. "Oh, you are lucky," Suzy said. "He is a fine teacher and the class will be super." "I dunno," the boy replied. "I didn't understand a single word he said today."

Instead of disappointing, such stories free me from the anxiety of influence. Society is addicted to tracking influence, so much so that we have all come to believe in it without thinking, no matter our experiences to the contrary. Sometimes when I can't think clearly and imagination half creates the world about me, I assume my essays influence people. About the time I begin to imagine myself a maker and shaker, perhaps even Emersonian in wisdom, a reader rescues me. "So that you will know what is on the minds of your readers, I am enclosing a slip of paper I found in one of your books in the Gainesville Library," a man wrote from Florida. Three inches wide and five inches tall, the paper was pink. Written neatly in pencil atop one side was "take chicken out of freezer."

After the appearance of *Dead Poets Society*, people associated me with John Keating, the teacher in the film, this despite my pointing out that characters in films and books were fictions.

Repeatedly I explained that Keating was the creation of Tom Schulman, who wrote the screenplay, and not my creation, and whatever part of me that appeared in Keating was small. People hunting sources always bag game. Escaping identity with Keating was impossible. I received scores of letters. Because Keating was a nice guy, most letters were pleasant. A few, however, were salutary and kept me from forgetting my place beside the blackboard. From Canada "The Poorest—Humblest—Divine Magistrate King of All Mankind," or as he also called himself, "The Supreme Ruler of the Sacred Planet Earth," sent a four-page photocopied letter. "O You Intellectually and Morally Dishonest Thug of Humanity," the Ruler began mildly before working himself into the spirit of criticism and accusing me of being a degenerated, dehumanized product of "alcoholics, prostitutes, whores, homosexuals, lesbians, satans, sinners, and power-hungry criminals." Eventually the Ruler demanded that I hand over all my worldly goods to him to be distributed "amongst the poorest of this Sacred Planet Spaceship Earth."

In part teaching is performance—not a performance, however, to be applauded. Applause is addictive. Because applause diverts attention from learning, it corrupts. Because teachers strut and fret the boards in front of class, celebrity can attract them. My moment before the public exhausted and sometimes frightened me. From Norfolk, a man wrote saying I was his "mentor." "I was on the docks," he recounted, "reading Walt Whitman's poetry, and rain started to fall. It was a sign that I was destined to be a great poet. Soon I will come to Connecticut to sit at your feet." "I respond by return mail," I wrote in reply, "because unfortunately my feet will soon be out of Connecticut. By the time you receive this letter I will be in England. I am writing a book and must remain there for at least two years in order to do research." In conclusion I stated, "Your real mentor cannot be me or any stranger. Instead your mentor should be your imagination. Coupled with hard work, imagination brings success."

Despite daily public performances, teachers, like everyone else, live much of their lives in private. I put the man off because he seemed nuts, and I had small children. Of course publicity associated with the film also brought wonderful moments. "I was thrilled to see your name in the *Journal-Constitution* several months ago," a woman wrote from Atlanta. "I sent the clipping to my grandson, and he was impressed that I knew you." After telling me about her grandson, the woman ended, asking, "Do you ever get to Atlanta anymore? We'd love to see you. I remember fondly the time you lived in this house while in school at Emory University." At the time I had spent only two weekends in Atlanta in my life, and not only did I not attend Emory but I'd never visited the campus. For a moment I was not sure how to respond. I did not want to embarrass my correspondent, who seemed old and kind. Some time ago a reviewer described me as a person "not possessed of a sensibility that is needlessly trammeled by facts." All good teachers, indeed all successful husbands, wives, and parents, quickly learn to lie. "Your letter," I eventually began, "brought back wonderful memories of days long past." I complimented the woman on her grandson's successes, then concluded by thanking her for her "warm and gracious letter." To confuse one person with another is commonplace, but in the commonplace lies magic and happiness, both in and out of the classroom.

Myth of the Great Teacher

Dealing with people as individuals is wearing, and in the attempt to make living easier society quantifies and turns people into players in a social drama: among others, the screwball scientist, the WASP, the Hispanic, the reformed rake, the ingenue, the hero, the terrorist, the booze-swilling, backroom-boy politician, and the inspirational, life-changing teacher. Outside school, fiction often depicts this teacher as a fuddy-duddy and a bumbler. In stories, though, the classroom transforms, and waving chalk and books about his head the mythological teacher becomes a Pentecostal instructor who converts students and immerses them in uplift and inspiration. Lost in the fiction of the great teacher is not simply a flawed human being but common sense. "Greatness of soul," the essayist Montaigne wrote, "is not so much pressing upward and forward as knowing how to set oneself in order and circumscribe oneself. It regards as great whatever is adequate, and shows its elevation by liking moderate things better than eminent ones." In other words true greatness rejects the concept of great, discovering meaning and finding happiness in the ordinary.

Because of *Dead Poets Society,* I receive much mail. Not long ago a young teacher wrote me from Oklahoma. He said he was having trouble inspiring his third-grade class, and he wondered if he should stand on his desk and teach "like you did in *Dead Poets Society*." I winced on reading the letter. "If you stand on your desk, third-graders will probably think you have gone around the bend," I wrote. I told the man that if he taught older children and ever stood on his desk he had better know his subject well "or else the kids will eat you alive." I also told him to relax. "Don't worry so much and just have fun. Don't take the class too seriously. People who take themselves too seriously," I said, "often don't accomplish much." I wanted to write that movies were only movies, not life, but the subject was too big for a letter.

When I taught at Montgomery Bell Academy, I was twenty-four and had just spent two years at Cambridge. Hormones raced through me in spillways. I taught fifteen-year-olds, sweet children all, but still fifteen-year-olds, people with whom I could be friendly but not friends. Indeed for years I have advised students that "when somebody my age wants to be your friend, watch out." Once after I spoke at a prep school in Perth, Australia, two eleventh-graders approached me. "Mr. Pickering," they said in unison, "couldn't you be our friend? We would really like that." "No," I said. "I could be your teacher, not your friend. Being your teacher is much better." "For me as well as you," I thought. In any case at Montgomery Bell Academy I did stand on desks and climb out of windows. I did such things not so much to awaken the kids but to entertain myself. If I had fun, I suppose I thought, the boys would have fun, too, and maybe enjoy reading and writing more. Maybe they would look forward to class even on sunny days.

The effects of classroom doings are always mysterious, something that should be pounded, intellectually of course, into every legislator in the nation. Too often tests measure the ability to take tests and not much more. Years later one of the students who was in my class at MBA wrote about my teaching. One day, he recounted, when the boys showed up for class, the door was shut. When the students knocked, a voice said, "Come in, gentlemen." They entered, but I was not in sight. Only when I said, "Take your seats" did they realize I was under the desk. For the next fifty minutes I read Thoreau with "great gusto." "I will never forget his admonition taken from his day of reading Thoreau from under the desk," the man wrote. "Do not find when you come to die that you have not lived." The man graduated from the University of Tennessee then attended the Wharton School of Business at the University of Pennsylvania, after which he became a banker. The class that I taught from under the desk, just to see if I could control twenty fifteen-year-olds for an hour when I could not see them (I did) was, he stated, the most memorable class he had ever attended.

Perhaps the asinine has greater effects than the inspirational, at least in the classroom. Indeed when I see the word *inspirational,* I read carefully. Just before I left Australia four years ago, an aspiring teacher wrote me. "You have made an impact like the proverbial stone in the pond. It may have started as an influence on one, but has affected the course of events in many lives. This is what I find curious. How can one person inspire others? How can it be done in one lifetime?" *Inspiration* itself seems a word that people use when nothing else comes to mind. At worst the word forms part of the stock vocabulary of panhandlers and barkers peddling quack medicines, that is, politicians, motivators, and preachers selling cure-alls for the incurable. Or so I sometimes think. Teachers should banish inspiration from their minds and labor to be competent and kind.

Oddly, and life is wonderfully odd, sometimes the unkind plays a big part in people's fondest memories of school. My grandfather Samuel Pickering grew up in Carthage, Tennessee, the real town, not the one sketched in my essays. At the end of the nineteenth century, the Carthage elementary school was small. Rumor swirled about the man who taught Grandfather. He had come to Carthage, children believed, from the Indian Territory, the land that later became Oklahoma. Children thought he had killed a man in the territory and had fled to Carthage to escape the hangman. In any case the teacher treated students harshly and was fond of switching boys. When a boy misbehaved, the teacher always sent another student outside to cut switches. Selecting switches was difficult. If a student cut weak switches, the teacher became mad at him. If the switches were too thick and strong, the boy being punished became angry. One day Henry Fisher misbehaved, and the teacher sent Grandfather outside to fetch switches. Grandfather said he picked the switches carefully. When he returned to the class, the teacher fondled the switches lovingly, turning them over and over in his hands. "Sammy," he eventually said, "these are the best switches I have ever seen, much too good for the likes of Henry Fisher, but just right for a good boy like you." "Whereupon," Grandfather recounted, shaking his head and laughing, "he whaled the tar out of me and made my legs bleed, even though I had done nothing wrong."

Cant grows thicker around education than learning. For years students have walked into my classes expecting the Great Teacher. Expectation, alas, determines what they see. In class I struggle to startle and awaken. I want students to escape platitude, if only for a moment. I want reaction to me to invigorate and so provoke them into thought that they grow beyond me. I fail. Escaping platitudinous behavior and thought is impossible, in part, of course, because such behavior may be decent and good. All teachers receive warm letters from former students. The first few letters we receive brighten days, but then we begin to notice the letters are similar. Instead of thinking about us and our classes, students have tumbled into a pattern of behavior. The letters I receive invariably begin, "You don't remember me but." Then follows a tribute, an account of life lived, and a conclusion promising, "I will never forget you."

Like preaching, effective teaching depends in part upon performance. Not all, but many good teachers are conjurers, delivering soliloquies, creating props with words, their voices pulling a cast of supporting characters into the classroom. For me dissatisfaction frequently accompanies the bell at the end of class. Once students vanish down the hall, I see myself as the poor player, strutting in front of children, not adults, a manipulator, not an educator or an ordinary guy fumbling through thought in order to explain or describe. Usually I feel worse when students think my classes best. At such times receiving a good letter is tonic, something that reassures and for a flicker of time makes me think myself not a complete fraud. "One time I wrote a poem for your class and apologized for it," a woman wrote. "You wrote back a note that I have always kept. Do your best, you said, and say no more. The advice has made all the difference to me over the years."

Despite such moments, praise is formulaic. At the final day of class this past December a student gave each member of my course a pamphlet entitled "Pickeringisms," fourteen pages of things I'd said during the semester. Many statements were vulgar; others were silly. Instead of provoking students to anger and thought, my remarks evoked affection and the choric "we will never forget you." No person escapes the time in which he lives. As I read the pamphlet I winced, seeing that Homeland Security had made me paranoid, imagining plots everywhere. "Bible Sunday Schools are training grounds for evangelical terrorists." "No poet ever celebrates nostrils. Do you know why?" I asked before lowering my voice and saying, "the Communists." Occasionally I commented on the fashionable and criticized society. "Any man over forty with a ponytail is a jackass." "I've never attended a cocktail party in the South without hearing people dying of laughter over someone's death."

What enriches a teacher's life, what enriches the lives of most people, are the small appointments of days, the details of which people try to remember but which ultimately slip from memory. To be sure nice letters from former students brighten the mail, but teachers ought to jettison thoughts about reputation or celebrity. I can name all the teachers who taught me, but I have forgotten their classes. Indeed much as childhood memories are fabrics of stories told to us by parents and relatives, so what I know about my first teachers comes from my parents. According to Mother, when I began to read I read from right to left, not left to right. "Don't worry," Miss Courtney, my first-grade teacher, told Mother. "I will straighten his reading out." She did. In old age Miss Courtney, like most of us, became a little strident, particularly when driving. According to story she refused to pause at four-way stop signs, saying there was no need for her to pause if everyone else stopped. After two crashes she lost her license.

Mr. Bass taught me in the sixth grade at Parmer School. Parmer has vanished, and I recall little about Mr. Bass, but I remember the eraser game. On rainy days when we could not go outside for recess, the class played the eraser game. Two children played at a time, the chaser and the chased. Both had blackboard erasers on their heads. Through the aisles they scurried, one pursuing the other until somebody's eraser fell off or the person being chased was tagged. Twelve years ago when they reached fifty years old, my Parmer classmates held a reunion at a resort in Alabama. During the day, some fished; others played tennis. At night, however, during the banquet, they played the eraser game.

"I remember the Twinkie Lady from kindergarten," a student told me. The woman taught special education. When the

woman had lunch duty, she strolled through the cafeteria looking for children who had brought Twinkies from home for dessert. When she saw a child with a Twinkie, she seized the
Twinkie and, after squeezing some of the filling onto her right
index finger, wiped the cream down along the child's nose,
making a white stripe. "We loved the game," the girl said, "and
whenever people had Twinkies, they made sure they were in
clear view so the Twinkie Lady would find them." "When I
was five years old, I peed my pants," another girl told me. "That
is what I remember best. I was sitting at a round table with my
kindergarten class. Jason Millman was to my left and Joan Conti
was directly across from me. Ms. Pender was standing in the
center of the room teaching us about the life and accomplishments of George Washington."

Lives are thick fabrics of experience, but few occupations
can match that of teaching. Many of my happiest memories occurred in the world surrounding teaching, not in the classroom
itself. I am comfortable in wrinkled and frayed clothes. When I
was a graduate student, I looked like a walking used-clothing
store. One morning after I had been at Princeton for four months,
the head janitor of the Graduate College appeared at my door.
In his arms he held a bundle of clothes. "Sam," he began, "I know
what it is like to be poor and not have good clothes. I lost everything during the war, and when I came to this country from
Latvia, people were wonderful. They gave me clothes and got
me this job. I now own a house, and both my children have
graduated from college. You remind me," he continued, "of

myself when I first came here, and I want you to have these clothes." The man's generosity was wondrous, and after thanking him profusely I took the clothes. The problem was that I was over six feet tall and skinny, and he was five-eight and fat. When I put his trousers on, the seat hung down like a watermelon, and the front pouched out like a leg of lamb. The legs stopped three inches above my ankles, but all this was a small matter when compared to the way his sweater fit. It gathered about my neck like a football player's shoulder pads, and then after hanging down for four or so inches, it bunched up over my chest, giving me a formidable bosom. Of course how the clothes fit was beside the point. What mattered were the man's generosity and his feelings. I had to wear the clothes, and wear them I did, at least twice a week until the janitor retired two and a half years later.

The niceness of such a story nearly brings a tear to the eye. As I have aged, I have grown sappy—paradoxically hard and sappy at the same time. Last year a friend with whom I have long taught told me he was dedicating his new book to me. I did not know what to say. Instead I went to my office, shut the door, and cried out of happiness. Of course not all the memories that furnish the lives of teachers are sentimental. Oddly enough many of the educational experiences that stick to mind are funny and, to use a contemporary word, inappropriate. Vicki's father attended Princeton. He had a robust sense of humor, and the stories he told about his undergraduate days were merry. When Vicki's father was a senior, a French professor invited him to his house for dinner. The man raised the meal like a well-wrought garden, each dish a well-tended bed blending harmoniously with the previous course. Just before dessert the man excused himself from the table and went into his bedroom. He was gone some time, and Vicki's father assumed he was fetching a tray of liqueurs. Vicki's father was mistaken. As he sat back in his chair, mulling the delights of Drambuie and Grand Marnier, the professor suddenly appeared in the doorway to the dining room. He was, as the British would put it, completely starkers. "Around the table and through the house he chased me," Vicki's father recounted. Vicki's father escaped with both honor and sense of humor intact. He said nothing about the evening. A month later a friend came to see him. The professor had invited the friend to dinner. The professor struck the boy as strange, and knowing that Vicki's father had eaten at the professor's house he asked if he should accept the invitation. "By all means," Vicki's father said emphatically, "the man is a magnificent cook, and the evening will be a night to remember. Dessert in particular will be an astonishing surprise."

As a teacher you will make a good living, but you will not become wealthy in financial terms. Beyond getting and spending, you will amass glittering moments. These will more than compensate for a modest income. Only the narrow and the naive are consistent, however. Although I have urged you not to overvalue tributes, sometimes notes and letters "make" a day, a week, or even a year. Two decades ago I spent a year teaching in Syria. The year was not easy. At the time I had not dropped the reins of ambition. Work that I wanted to do was shunted off to others, and I fretted that opportunity had passed me by. I fretted, that is, until the last day of class when a girl handed me a poem she had written. Suddenly the year seemed glorious. "Like the effect of sunset," she wrote, "Like the gone of the moon, / Like shadwos spreading in space, / Like storms which destroy everything / Like all these things your leaving will be. / Your leaving will fill our hearts with sadness and dullness. / Your leaving will take the dynamic thing from our life. / Maybe my swords is very big for the situation, / But that is really what I feel and the truth / So you have a right by getting back home again, / But we haven't the right to possess whom we loved. / God help you with your coming life. / God take care of you and your wife fore ever. / I want of you just to remember that there are / Students loves you and think of you forever."

"Shadwos" spread through all lives, and as sunny as teaching can be, dark moments abound. When I first started teaching in college at Dartmouth, I had a study on the third floor of the library. Four doors down from me, an emeritus professor named Haynie Givner had a study. Every day when I came in after class Haynie was at work. Three years passed, and then one morning Haynie came into my study. His shoulders were hunched over, and tears ran down his face. "Sam," he sobbed, "I don't know what to do. This morning I finished my book." "Haynie," I said, "that's splendid." "No," he answered, "you are too young and don't understand. For six years I have worked on the book. If the publisher rejects it, I will have worked six years for nothing. But if he accepts it, I won't have anything left to do, and my life will be over." I still don't have an answer for Haynie, at least not one that will satisfy him, or me. Ours is a problem-solving age in which people believe that if only they can find the right key any problem can be solved. The truth is not all problems are locks that can be opened, and maybe that is part of the wonder of living. You must recognize that much lies beyond your knowledge and skills.

Letter Two: The Good Teacher

DEAR TEACHER,

As you know good teachers are not always good people. While some successful teachers are saints, others are sinners. Most are ordinary people, however, doing their best to get through life decently. Generally good teachers behave well, though, being human, of course, they often fail, sometimes spectacularly. I have been interviewed often about educational matters. The questions asked are similar. Interviewers start by asking, "What teachers influenced you?" Form determines content. Because most interviews are published in newspapers, writers don't have space enough to ruminate. Consequently I usually give writers what their question implies and mention one or two teachers, good people to be sure but not the shapers of my life. The truth is that home, heredity, and luck, lots of luck, not a single year with one teacher, have determined the course of my life. The question that ought to be asked is what teachers did I influence. Was fourth grade ever the same for Miss Bonny after I left, and how did I change Mrs. Harris's life in eighth grade?

The next question reporters ask is invariably, "What makes a good teacher?" Usually I shift the topic. Despite teaching institutes and libraries of research, there is no satisfactory answer. Blended in a good teacher are knowledge and personality. Both knowledge and personality are various, however, and the blend is mysterious and volatile. The person who is a wonderful teacher at thirty may be terrible at forty then good again at fifty-five. Life can wear people down then turn around the next year and invigorate them. Problems arise and vanish. The teacher who stirs the top quarter of the class might not be effective with the lower quarter. Moreover, students often don't recognize good teaching until they have left school. The teacher who seemed incandescent to the fifteen-year-old can appear irresponsible from the perspective of middle age. Likewise the teacher damned as dull and unimaginative by twenty-year-olds might be praised as challenging and provocative by the same people when they become forty-year-olds.

Despite knowledge and preparation, the success of a class may depend more upon your mood, not something stressed in teaching institutes or in most classes taken by prospective teachers. In the past I often swam before class. One morning as I was leaving the pool, I noticed an older faculty member walk out of the men's locker room, step on the tile, and stride toward me. Over his shoulders hung a red towel. The towel was gathered neatly and was almost dashing. Clearly the man arranged it carefully. In his left hand he carried a striped athletic bag. The man's air was jaunty, and he was pleased with himself. Unfortunately, he had forgotten to put on his bathing suit. "Well," I greeted him as he approached, "aren't you the bold lad?" He looked puzzled, and I continued, "You are doing something I have wanted to do but have never been able to muster the nerve for."

When he looked irritated, almost contemptuous at my unexpected familiarity, I said, "Only a real man would be brave enough to come out here bare ass and fancy free." An hour later my class was a success. I was in high good spirits that nothing could dampen.

Not all unexpected events are so jolly and lift mood and class. Some time back the local newspaper interviewed me. My birthday was mentioned in the article. Monday when I was in a nearby café, pouring half-and-half into a coffee mug, a stranger introduced himself. "We have the same birthday," he said, "September thirtieth. Have you ever thought," he continued, "that you were conceived on New Year's Eve and your parents were probably drunk as hell?" Although the thought had never crossed my mind, it beat a path through my brain during class thirty minutes later. No matter what students said I could not push the picture of Mother and Father out of my imagination, eyes glazed, tossing streamers to the ceiling, little red party hats falling down over their ears.

I don't want to reduce successful teaching to happenstance. Much of what you have learned in school will be useful, especially when you begin teaching. But the teaching life and teachers themselves are more various than any school can describe. From Sewanee I carted away good grades, a love of reading, and memories of teachers—more memories than ideas. My favorite teacher was playful but unconscionably biased and irresponsible. He was a segregationist. He brought copies of the *National Geographic* to class and, holding up pictures of African natives gamboling on riverbanks, said bitingly, "These people want to go to school with you." Hardly a day passed during which he did not lambaste Germans, Catholics, and teetotalers. He taught Romantic poetry, but he didn't talk much about poems. Yet the poets we read in his class clung to mind. Even today I can quote long passages of Wordsworth and Byron, something that for some strange reason makes me think better of the world.

While more responsible and diligent teachers, men and women who labored for truth and right, have almost vanished from memory, I remember this man vividly—and fondly. When my roommate Ed received a B in the man's course, he went to the professor's office. "Mr. Eaton," he said, "I made A's on all the tests and yet you gave me a B. That can't be correct." "Just a minute, poor boy," Mr. Eaton said and rummaged through a file. He pulled out a lined card and showed it to Ed. "Hatch, here are the midterm grades from all your other courses. You had B's in them. You are not an A student." "But Mr. Eaton," Ed responded, "I got A's in those courses for the semester." "Hatch," he said, peering over his glasses, "you are not lying, are you?" "No, sir," Ed replied. "I made A's." "Oh, dear," Mr. Eaton said, picking up a pencil and writing a note. "I have made a mistake. Take this to the registrar." Ed got his A with little trouble; the registrar had seen many notes like his.

Use of Education

What you do in the classroom is important, oddly often more important for yourself than for your students. People forever struggle to quantify the effects of education, pointing out, for example, how much more money a college graduate will make over his lifetime than a nongraduate. What is important is not how much money one makes but what one does with an education, and a life. Religion has not reformed human nature, and neither will education. Distrust utilitarians who quantify and attempt to reduce success and failure to numbers. Numbers will never justify existence. Indeed most of the things you and I think important, and dear, cannot be quantified: a child's holding your hand and saying, "You are the best daddy in the world," a field of dandelions in the spring, the serrated edge of hatred, a cold day in a graveyard white with snow, in short almost all the things that stitch lives into tapestries. By all means teach skills, reading and writing, for they are important. But resist the urge to inflate what you do. Whenever my thoughts float up from the good black earth and I imagine myself a molder of the future, old tales purge my mind.

In Carthage the Pankeys were a "twisty mouth family." While the faces of Everlena and Sister Sue Pankey twisted to the left, those of Pappy Farrell and Big Billy Pankey twisted so far to the right that the openings for their mouths seemed tracheotomies drilled under ears instead of beneath chins. In contrast to the rest of the family, the mouth of Jefferson Davis, the youngest of the Pankeys, was normal. Moreover, unlike his family, Jefferson Davis was bright. After graduating from high school in Carthage, he attended Austin Peay State University in Clarksville in hopes of becoming an elocution teacher. At the end of Jefferson Davis's first semester, the Pankeys had a homecoming party for their son. Everlena put the big pot in the little pot, even setting candles on the table. At the end of the meal Everlena turned to her husband and said, "Pappy, would you blow the candles out?" Pappy leaned over the table and blew vigorously. Instead, though, of streaming forward over the candles, air billowed out of his mouth to the right. "Mammy, you better try," he said, getting red in the face. Everlena had no more success than Farrell, her breath shooting out to the left. Eventually she asked Big Billy to blow the candles out. Next Sister Sue tried. Finally the family turned to Jefferson Davis and asked him to blow out the candles. Little J.D., as they sometimes called him, sat up in his chair and with one breath extinguished the flames. "What a blessed thing it is to have learning," Pappy said, beaming at Mammy.

Having an education does bless days. For a teacher, having a sense of humor is also important. Not only will humor brighten your hours, but it can deflect the unpleasant. A good teacher must be able to delight in others and life itself, even aspects that are not readily appealing. Good teachers must also be able to slip leashes binding them to tests and justification. In our fallen educational world, you have to teach to tests imposed by legislators and theorists who sentimentalize the bad old times of the basics and who sometimes believe education dangerous because learning does not necessarily support society as it is. People who cannot manage a single marriage, much less their own children, believe they can manage education, or, for that matter, nature, even the world. Not long ago I received a letter from a man demanding, not asking, that I justify teaching English. I sent him an excerpt from one of my books, a description of a side-show in Carthage. Causing a sensation was "The World's Smallest Giant." People flocked to view the "monster." "He was only five feet eight inches tall," Loppie Groat told the crowd at a local café. "What was amazing was that he looked like a nor-mal fellow. If there hadn't been a sign over his cage, I would have passed right by." "That shows the importance of educa-tion," Googoo Hooberry added. "If you hadn't been able to read, you wouldn't have knowed he was a giant, and you'd have missed a once-in-a-lifetime sight."

Justifications are quicksand. The more you write trying to explain the benefits of education without leaning upon numbers the deader and more inaccurate your language will become. In the attempt to avoid controversy, you will write boilerplate. That is why colleges rely so heavily on slogans, declaring, for example, "We Are Committed to Excellence." If you are not being ex-amined for continuation or tenure, cobble together a short state-ment, drop it like a board atop the sand, skip across the veneer, and get back to teaching and living. In the case of tenure, you must behave differently. Establishments, if not necessarily the people who compose them, are impressed by thick folders. When being considered for continuation, stir yeast into all your accom-plishments and thoughts and let them rise so that they fill shelves. Write a statement detailing your "philosophy" of education, even though you spend days coping, not pondering. Quote famous educators and writers. Include detailed study plans, assignment sheets, and sample tests. After you finish, read a diverting mystery, something, oddly enough, that probably has more to do with actual life than what you just put together.

Still, when you can, be brief. In September I was asked to write two pages describing the purpose of an English major. I wrote two sentences. "A major in English ought to brighten students' days by awakening then nurturing a fondness for and an interest in words and reading. English should teach students to read critically, that is, be able to understand not merely how stories and poems are made, but how words can create worlds." Social conservatives should, of course, suspect education. Learning like ignorance undermines vested interests. On the other hand a little learning, but not too much, stabilizes society, in the name of order and right buttressing existing injustice and evil. Ten years ago while I was driving Eliza to soccer practice, she asked, "Daddy, what is Communism?" "Communism was," I said, "a theory of government. Like all theories it promised people better lives." I explained that the gap between theory and practice was vast, primarily, I said, because humans were flawed creatures. Self always gets in the way when people try to implement theory. "Instead of our brothers' keepers," I said, "we become our brothers' exploiters. Communism," I continued, promised "a fairer distribution of income. If the United States were a Communist country, I would not have the money to send you to camp in Maine each summer. But then maybe some of the poor children in Hartford would have better lives." "That doesn't sound bad to me," Eliza said. "I don't know why Americans hate Communism so much."

I didn't say anything else. Since the practice field was four miles from our house, I stayed at practice and talked to parents. Most parents were threads from the same financial and social fabric: doctors, teachers, lawyers, and artists. A few parents did not have means, however. On the weekend Eliza's team was scheduled to play in a tournament. The entrance fee for each child was fifteen dollars. "Is Sally looking forward to the tournament?" I said to a mother. "She'd like to play," the woman answered slowly, "but we can't come up with the fifteen dollars. Bill broke his arm six weeks ago. He hasn't worked since, and we don't have insurance." Sally played in the tournament. Afterward she baked me an apple pie. The pie was sweet. Still, as I ate it, my mind scrolled back to the conversation with Eliza. "Fifteen dollars," I thought, "from each according to his abilities. To each according to his need." Then I sliced thought off. Edward had a sore throat and a temperature of 102. I had a set of freshman papers to grade and a mound of bills to pay for an uncle in a nursing home.

Students and You

During the first year we spent in Australia, Eliza was eight years old. Schools did not assign much homework, and she had leisure enough to teach herself. Day after day she wrote stories, one of which she called, "What Tommy Grasshopper Saw." The story was short. "When Tommy Grasshopper jumped, he saw fields with horses running over them, trout swimming in rivers, a fox playing in a pine forest, and an eagle circling round a mountain. He saw a lot in just one glance before he fell." As a teacher you inhabit a kaleidoscopic world. Each day brings astonishing sights, or at least it will if you are alert. Before you fall, you will have lived through an almost infinite variety of experiences. Amid the variety are, I think, several constants. When I first started teaching, an emeritus professor said, "Sam, if you think the best of people, they will give you their best." That may be the most useful advice I have ever received. I make myself think the best of students. Sometimes trusting and encouraging are not easy. Still, the good teacher must trust. Only rarely have students taken advantage of me. Students are, however, very different from you. Among the mistakes teachers make is trying so hard to "relate" to students that they become almost teenagers themselves. In fact banish the word *relate* from your vocabulary. Keep in touch with your inner adult. Unlike the inner child, the inner adult inhabits the brain not the bowel.

Instead of becoming a devotee of popular culture, expose students to what they are not familiar with, in particular high art and music. Students inhabit popular culture. Treat them to High Culture, even to "high seriousness." "Mr. Pickering," a student said to me last year, "don't you realize there is a generation gap, maybe two gaps, between you and our class?" "Oh, no," I said, widening my eyes. "I can't believe that." The truth is that in addition to teaching writing and reading, math and science, you should expose students to difference. Children grow by comparing the familiar with the unfamiliar. Be what you are rather than what you think students want you to be. As you age, you will discover that you believe less and marvel more, something that will separate you from students. No matter how you struggle, you will not know your students well. When my children were young, I read to them for an hour a day, seven days a week for nine years. One night as I read to her in bed, Eliza turned toward me and interrupted, saying, "There are many things you don't know about me." "What?" I said, looking up from my book. "I don't know how to explain," Eliza said, talking more to herself than to me. "Even though you have lived with me for seven years and are my daddy there is a lot you don't know about me."

Am I implying that you should remain distant from students? No; celebrate their joys. Cushion their griefs. Help them to dream. Teach them. But realize age has separated you from them. When they were in the womb, parents whispered, "What do you want to be?" Not a grade goes past without someone creating anxiety for them by asking such questions. I, and maybe you, grew up in a different time. Only once has anyone ever asked me what my goals were, and that was at an interview for a college presidency. "Aside from seduction," I said, "I haven't had a goal since I was seventeen. I have outgrown goals. All I want now is to get through the years ahead without hurting people." I did not become president of the college.

Clever teachers make differences between them and their students interesting and educational. "My favorite elementary school teacher was Irish," a student told me. "Every morning he greeted the class, saying, 'Top o' the morning.' After we said,

'Top o' the morning to you,' he whacked his desk three times with a shillelagh, and lessons began. I never enjoyed studying so much, and I never learned so much." The children learned in part not only because the teacher made his difference a source of interest and delight but also because he was lively. "Every spring after the rains began," the student told me, "he organized Earthworm Day, the highlight of which was the Grand National Earthworm Race."

Of course, by being teachers we have in a sense become corporate, and along with lessons about Irish culture and earthworms, along with making students look forward to class, we have to provide students with credentials that too often pass for real learning. As a result amid high hopes for sweetness and light we must blend the practical, that is, teach toward examinations.

Mind you, what is real is another matter, one that you must not let undermine or confuse you. Instead let it amuse. "Daddy," my son said at breakfast many years ago, "was God real when the dinosaurs were real?" "Absolutely," I said, "no question about it. God created the dinosaurs." The answer satisfied Edward, but it did not satisfy me. Little in my life seemed absolute or, for that matter, real, not even breakfast itself. Gone from my life were days freshened by bug and worm, tomatoes from the garden, and corn pone fried in bacon grease. In front of me was a pale tablet of extra-strength Ascriptin, containing "50% more Aspirin plus Maalox," and two gels, a round one twice as big as a BB containing three milligrams of garlic oil in a base of soybean oil but equivalent to fifteen hundred milligrams of fresh

garlic, and then a long gel resembling a miniature yellow diri-
gible, filled with a thousand milligrams of concentrated fish oil,
extracted from, the label stated, the marine lipid. Covering my
cereal, an all-natural granola, were wheat germ and brewer's
yeast, the whole awash in skim milk. Steaming in the mug to
my right was not boiled coffee, lumps of thick cream floating
about the top like white islands, but caffeine-free tea. "Yes,
Edward," I repeated, "God was real then, and He's real now.
He made the dinosaurs, and He makes everything except what
I eat for breakfast each morning." The tests around which you
are forced to raise much of your curriculum may strike you as
unreal, bubble sheets that measure little. Still, good teachers will
always find ways to make preparing for tests enjoyable for students, if not satisfying for themselves.

We are very different from the children we teach. Charac-
teristics we admire in adults don't necessarily become children.
In an essay entitled "On Vagabonds," the nineteenth-century
Scottish essayist Alexander Smith wrote, "We do not love a man
for his respectability, his prudence and foresight in business, his
capacity for living within his income at his banker's. . . . The
things that really move liking in human beings are the gnarled
nodosities of character, vagrant humours, freaks of generosity,
some little unextinguishable spark of the aboriginal savage, some
sweet savour of the old Adam." A class of Adams gnawing apples
and fondling Eves rather than books would make most of us bolt
for the reptile house at the zoo. Children are irrational and moody.
Of course adults are irrational also, but they are less spontaneously

so, usually thinking a second or two before they say or do stupid things. My friend Harry's son Phil turned fifteen in January. For years Harry had been the devoted father, carting Phil across New England to countless athletic events. Together they cooked dinner, delighting in pastas and cakes. Phil's wish was Harry's command. Near the end of January I met Harry on the sidewalk outside the university gymnasium. He looked glum. "What's the matter, old fellow?" I said, adding, "How's Phil?" "Phil," Harry said dolefully, "is different. Last night I wanted to talk to him about school. I went upstairs to his room and sat next to him on the edge of his bed. Before I could open my mouth, Phil glared at me and said, 'Do you practice being an asshole?'"

John Locke convinced the eighteenth century that education shaped adults and determined children's futures, both moral and financial, a belief that buttresses education today. The next six years will civilize Phil, teaching him craft and stratagem. He will become an amiable hypocrite like most adults, and his language will wax smooth. In dark moments I sometimes think that colleges function primarily as day-care centers for postadolescents. Under the guise of bestowing knowledge and credentials, colleges confine youth driven reckless by hormones, preventing the young from disrupting society. Indeed upon graduation students are so burdened by debt that they are forced into conventional patterns of behavior. By the time they pay off their student loans, they have aged into being safely corporate.

If you cannot be buddies with your students, you can certainly enjoy their successes, not all of which will or should be academic. One of my first college students was named Pixie. Although she had a smile like Christmas in the country, she spent an unhappy first term in college. Her parents telephoned every night to see if she was in her room. In the dormitory, her nicest intentions turned sour. When she cooked fudge for her floor mates, she left out the sugar. I couldn't do much about the fudge. But I did manage to sweeten her family on Parents' Weekend. They came to my home for sherry, and as we chatted, I said, "Pixie seems unhappy. When such a good girl is unhappy, the world is out of joint." The telephone calls stopped, and one bright morning as I walked across the college green, I heard a girl cry, "Professor Pickering! Professor Pickering!" Pixie came running across the grass. "Professor," she burst out when she reached me, "the most wonderful thing has happened. I think I'm in love."

Students enrich our lives in all sorts of ways, some of which are remarkably silly or odd. Sometimes students attach notes to their examinations, a practice I discourage. "Professor," Adam wrote, disobeying my instructions, "I'd like to thank you for teaching me so much about writing. Normally when I write this kind of letter at the end of a blue book I'm just kissing ass. But I want you to know that I'm not kissing your ass. I am trying to be sincere here. I really did learn a lot about writing." Ross, another student, described building a sweat hut. "I started the task," he said, "by asking each rock if he or she would like to participate in the ceremony. Having lived in the deafening Western culture for the past decade, I am no longer able to hear the whispers of my brother rocks and trees. I know they try to make me hear, and so I talk to them. I made sure not to take any rocks that preferred to avoid the ceremony." "Is Ross around the bend?" Vicki asked after I read her the description of building the hut. "No," I said. "He just communicates with the world in ways beyond most people. Anyway, he writes clearly. Of course, if he brought a family of rocks to class, set them on his desk, and started talking to them, that would be different. I don't like being interrupted by people or rocks."

On other occasions students remind us of the mixed nature of life, something that makes good teachers want to do better by and for humanity. When Ali missed a week of classes at the University of Jordan, he came to my office and apologized. He had been in Lebanon. Phalangists had overrun his village, he explained, and killed twelve members of his family, seven men and five women. As the oldest surviving male, he had to arrange the burials. Shrugging his shoulders, he looked out the window for a moment then turned to me and said, "Christians kill Moslems. Moslems kill Christians. That's life."

Students may make teachers aware of injustice, and the sadness of students' lives should invigorate us. Rarely, however, do students teach us much intellectually. One of the sappy questions you will hear several times during your career is, "What have students taught you?" Questioners want and expect an answer airborne with uplift in which words such as *energy* and *creativity* flare brightly. Give people the answer they want, then get on to other matters. Once after I addressed a group of parents, a father asked me the question. I made the mistake of being honest.

"Nothing," I said. "I am fifty years old, and my students are eighteen. Even if they had something to teach me, I would not want to learn it." For days afterward I fumed, dissatisfied with myself because I had been unnecessarily harsh. Along with telling white lies, teachers should learn the proper use of the superlative. The more teachers praise and celebrate, decorating conversations with superlatives, the freer they will be to teach their subjects and the less they will have to regret. And certainly students do occasionally teach us, though what we learn usually is not as elevating as parents want to think.

Long after rebuffing the father, I remembered something I had learned, not the stuff of the old educational shell game, a pink inspirational response, but the sinew and gristle of real learning. From Ian, now in vet school, I learned "the recto-vaginal technique of artificially inseminating cattle." "All the books we have read about nature are fine but abstract," Ian said one day after I lectured on John Muir. "What you need is hands-on experience." Hands-on turned out to be hands-in. That afternoon I met Ian in the university dairy barn. Over my left arm I put a plastic sleeve. Thirty-seven inches long, the sleeve reached from shoulder to fingertips. Loose fitting, the sleeve was ten and a half inches wide at the shoulder while the distance between the end of the thumb and that of the little finger was eleven inches. Ian demonstrated the technique on a Holstein. The cow was skittish, so he suggested I practice on another of "the ladies," a quiet Jersey with a plastic identity tag stapled through her left ear. Printed on the tag were the name

Cheryl and the number 874. I lubricated the end of the glove with soap and water. Afterward I pushed my fingers together into an arrowhead and leaning against Cheryl eased my hand into her rectum. For a moment Cheryl tensed, and her muscles contracted, squeezing my arm. Soon, though, she relaxed, and my arm slipped deep inside her. I, too, relaxed. As I rubbed the base of her tail, heat from her body washed through my arm, eroding and softening the sharp pain of arthritis.

"If you can't find me," I told my friend Josh, the next day, "look in the dairy barn. I will be up to my shoulders in arthritis cure-all." In order to find the cervix, which lay just under the "rectal floor," I scooped several handfuls of manure out of Cheryl. "Once you get that field butter out," Ian instructed, "push down and you will discover the cervix. It feels like a turkey neck." In my right hand I held a foot-and-a-half-long plastic rod with a plunger at one end and, if I had really been fertilizing Cheryl, a dollop of sperm at the other. Carefully I inserted the rod into the vagina. The going wasn't easy. I steered a slow course, but eventually I tacked through the rings of the cervix and docked at the uterine horns. "Nothing to it," I told friends the next morning in a local café. "Give me a cup of coffee and bring on the whole damn herd." Never, by the by, underestimate the ignorance of the partially learned, that is, all of us. "Artificial insemination? Did I hear correctly?" a woman asked after I left for class. "It won't take. He is a human, and the cow's body will reject it. He is a teacher. He ought to know better."

Letter Three: Qualities of a Teacher

DEAR TEACHER,

Even though, as I hinted earlier, some successful teachers are misanthropic, I suspect the most important quality of a good teacher is the capacity to like people. Despite forever having to grade, you must be able to suspend judgment and appreciate people for what they are. You must be able to hold contrary views in your mind simultaneously, what literary critics call negative capability. No matter the occasional sharpness of your tongue, you should be so flexible that some folks will think you weak. I do not mean that you should become weakly tolerant, for there are many things in life that should never be tolerated. But you should be capable of compassion. You should be strong enough to be the Good Samaritan. Moreover do not waste much time analyzing yourself. Good teachers cope with what life thrusts at them and don't worry about small things like consistency. Many years ago I gave the final speech or benediction at a peace festival in Storrs. Two thousand schoolchildren attended. For class projects they invented peace games, board games in which winners overcame the urge to fight and won their ways to peace, not oil or money.

Several guests attended the festival. From the former Soviet Union came a young mother. She did not speak English, but she brought a game created by her nine-year-old daughter. Although uninvited, two "war activists" also appeared and handed out broadsheets urging that the United States withdraw from "the godless pro-Communist, and anti-American United Nations." They wandered about and were ignored until they discovered the Russian woman and began haranguing her. They did not harangue long. I handed my speech to a friend, and in the good cause of peace fired a salvo of hearty, salty language at the men. I urged them to decamp, threatening to thrash them into sudden bowel movements. They left, and twenty minutes later I gave my speech, preaching the importance of temperance and pacifism. "Good Lord," Vicki exclaimed when I told her what happened. "You threatened to beat the shit out of two people at a peace festival? Isn't that a little inconsistent?" "You bet," I said, "and it was the right thing to do."

Optimism

Optimism oozes out of children's books like sap from maples in the spring. In *The Little Engine That Could,* a small blue engine pulls a train of toys and goodies over a mountain, puffing, "I think I can. I think I can." When Mayzie the lazy bird forsakes her nest, Horton sits faithfully on the egg, enduring ridicule, storms, and being shipped across the sea to be exhibited in a circus. Horton's virtue is rewarded when the egg cracks and an elephant bird appears, takes flight, then settles lovingly on Horton's trunk. As much as we want to believe that the blue engine pulled the train over the mountain, older readers look at friends who have succumbed to alcohol, bad luck, illness, and living beyond their means and know that somewhere on the mountain the engine spun off the tracks, dumping cars and hopes down a steep cliff. From the long view of age, Horton seems almost a sap, faithful one hundred percent. We know that the egg addled and didn't hatch. In fairy tales Beauty's love transforms Beast into a beauty; a frog becomes a prince; David, an effete musician, kills a giant with a slingshot, a child's toy; and a kitchen slut who sleeps amid ashes by the hearth marries a prince. Often in fairy tales characters do not simply "Be All You Can Be," but they live existences rich almost beyond imagination.

In *Puss 'n Boots,* a cat overcomes an ogre through trickery. In many tales, *Jack and the Beanstalk,* for example, children triumph through trickery, in other words by using their brains. From one point of view, education enables children to overcome forces that threaten their futures and often their lives. *The History of Tommy Titmouse,* the title page of an eighteenth-century children's book states, is the biography of "A LITTLE BOY, who became a Great Man, by minding his Learning, doing as he was bid, and being good-natured and obliging to every Body." John Locke wrote that nine men out of ten were made good or evil, useful or not by their educations. Education has superceded fairy godmothers, at least in popular thought. With a good education, every person can rise from the hearth to a palace of his own making. No child will be left behind. Children are the fathers and mothers of the adults to come. With the proper education, that is, intervention early enough, all children can achieve almost unimagined happiness and success. Small blue engines develop inner strengths that enable them to climb mountains and achieve the impossible. The thought invigorates, and a teacher ought never to forsake belief in the transforming power of schooling. The problem is that like all beliefs this one is only partially true. Hours in school rarely compensate for the multiple failings of home and street, of heredity and luck. Schooling can ameliorate but it cannot erase completely.

Stories of impossible transformations offer hope and are the mundane copy of magazines like *Sports Illustrated* and *Cosmopolitan,* so much so that they become ripe for ridicule. Some time ago when E.W.B. Childers was fishing off the bridge over Difficult Creek near Carthage, he caught a small catfish with a white mark in the shape of a foot on its head. Normally E.W.B. threw little fish back, but the mark was unique, and he took the fish home to show to his wife Mae and their two boys, Juba and Origin. After showing it to the boys, E.W.B. was going to throw the fish out, but Origin had read about an aquarium in his school reader and he asked his father if he could keep the fish in a wash-tub in the woodshed. Mae didn't object, so E.W.B. tossed it into the tub, and for the rest of the summer Juba and Origin fed it, first worms and grasshoppers, then slops as the weather turned chilly. The fish ate everything: orange peels, chicken bones, and once, after Juba misbehaved and was sent away from the table before dessert, a piece of strawberry shortcake with whipped cream on top.

Throughout the winter the children played with the fish, dropping it on the ground many times. The fish was hardy, though, and thrived on exercise and kitchen leavings. By March it had grown so big that E.W.B. put it in the rain barrel. Jumping out of the barrel was easy, and by late spring the fish was spending more time out of water than in. On warm days it liked nothing better than stretching out in the grass and dozing. After a nap it often played tag with Dog, an old beagle who appeared at Childers's back door some years before, covered with cockleburs and ticks big as plums. Staying out on the grass for hours at a time gave the fish a huge appetite, and that summer it grew monstrously big eating turnip greens cooked with hog jowl, watermelon, corn on the cob, and apple turnovers. The fish had such an appetite that E.W.B. said he didn't know how he could keep it. Then one day in October he saw a poster for a catfish derby in Gordonsville, advertising a thirty-dollar prize for the biggest fish. E.W.B. reckoned he could win, and when the day of the derby arrived Ollie Harwell from next door helped him hoist the fish onto the wagon, and he set out for Gordonsville. All went well until he started across the bridge over Difficult Creek. Then because the wagon was so heavily laden one of the planks on the bridge cracked and the wagon tilted sideways, dumping the catfish into the creek, just at the spot where E.W.B. had originally caught it. As soon as the fish fell into the water, E.W.B. jumped out of the wagon and ran down to the bank to haul it out. Alas, before he could pull it onto shore the catfish drowned.

As the old saying puts it, "Most fish stories am fibious." But then most transformation tales are kindly fibs. What is crucial in the classroom, however, is that teachers, despite years having stripped extravagant expectation from their lives, fib enough to convey hope, not simply to students but to themselves, if only for a moment. Nothing, though, is simple. Beyond the classroom optimism can distort and be dangerous. "Maybe America is so brutal," my friend Josh said, "because Americans refuse to look hard at life and tell the truth. Instead of staring at the consequences of actions, Americans avert their eyes and gazing into cloudy dream far from shattered bone envision realities swollen with up-lift, buttressed by moral certitude." At its best, however, the class-room is a protected place in which hope ought to buoy lessons and lives. Never forget that children are not adults, not even twenty-year-old children. The optimism that may blind adults and cause hardship may open a child's eyes and lead to happiness.

I emphasize the importance of a teacher's being optimistic because teachers establish the tones of their classes. Happily, be-cause they are young and not yet able to shape the stories of their lives, or at least the endings, students are usually optimistic. For my short story class students write stories. No matter the season, no matter the turmoil in their lives, they invariably write opti-mistic stories, frequently about athletic doings. In a recent batch of tales, a girl swam to her personal best in two events as the university defeated "its archrival Syracuse." A long last-minute pass won a football game; a grand slam with two out in the ninth won a baseball game. A shy girl rode to acclaim in "Walk, Trot,

Equitation." To help his team, a football player changed from tackle to guard, risking a career in the National Football League. Selflessness was rewarded. The next summer the boy made the Colorado World Winds and at the end of his first season starred in the Super Bowl. Although his left arm was broken, J.R. refused to leave the baseball field. He remained at second base and made "a spectacular bare-handed grab," insuring Connecticut's victory in the Big East Championship game. For two years in high school Betsey worked to become as good a sprinter as her older sister Kathleen. Because Kathleen had led the school to the state championship and Betsey rarely placed in a meet, the coach thought "Betsey was dogging it." One day to punish her for doing poorly in a sprint, the coach entered her in the 3200. During the run, Betsey "blossomed, learning that she was not a sprinter but a distance runner." Not only did she win the race but she qualified for the state meet.

Surprise will invigorate you. A child who appears hopelessly mired down by life or the seeming absence of talent will suddenly split his shell and fly glittering to achievement. Henry Thoreau ended *Walden* optimistically by describing an insect gnawing its way out of a wooden table. The insect represented man, deadened by getting and spending, a child smothered by home and circumstance. "Who knows what beautiful and winged life, whose egg has been buried for ages under many concentric layers of woodenness in the dead dry life of society," Thoreau wrote, "may unexpectedly come forth amidst society's most trivial and handselled furniture, to enjoy its perfect summer life at last!"

What you should not forget is that in making school a protected place we have also made it artificial. Students who do well
in a limited number of subjects receive rewards. Beyond school,
children, and then adults, succeed in multiple ways. The Little
Tommy Titmouse who collected A's may fail once he strays
beyond the margins of tests. Nerds and Bad Boys often succeed
after school, Huck Finn being the prime example. In great part
Huck succeeds because he is uneducated and uneducatable. Because he does not know how to behave properly and with propriety, he behaves morally and decides not to write Miss Watson
and reveal the whereabouts of Jim, saying, "All right, then, I'll
go to hell." "The triumph of the nerds" resembles Cinderella and
is a fairy tale, one, though, that embodies enough truth for us
not to reject it. Every child has some talent, waiting to be discovered. Finding it, however, often takes great effort, and you
might not be able to do it.

A teacher must be patient and incredibly flexible. Occasionally I think a demon invented elementary and high school, lim-
ing days and caging youth like birds. Instead of sitting behind
desks and memorizing the capitals of states, something I loved,
maybe students should be outside eating worms and getting dirty
and scabby. Thinking about education should make you flexible
and understanding. Josh once said, "All truths are half wrong,
except for self-evident truths which are always three-quarters
wrong." One evening, according to a Palestinian story, Truth
bathed in the Jordan River. Busy scrubbing off the tarnish of the
world, Truth did not see Falsehood creeping through willows

above the riverbank. Falsehood filched Truth's clothes. After slipping them on and tossing his own rags into reeds, Falsehood vanished, taking the road to Nablus. When Truth discovered his clothes were missing, he pursued Falsehood. In the stolen clothes, Falsehood was well turned out, wearing stylish made-to-order words, looking to the truth born. On meeting Falsehood, people embraced him and welcomed him into homes and lives. Because Truth was naked, villagers shunned him and, throwing kitchen slops and camel dung at him, chased him from village to village.

Unless you live closeted, and no teacher does, adaptability is necessary to the teaching life. You will be asked to teach things about which you know little. Give them a whirl. The new subjects might be fun. Blowing fresh through your classroom, they might make you energetic. Staying ahead of children is easy, particularly in general knowledge courses. Specialist courses, complicated classes in chemistry, for example, or music or involved mathematics, are another matter. When asked to teach something that terrifies you, bleat and run. Years ago in one of my books Judge Rutherford interviewed Proverbs Goforth for a teaching post in Carthage. When the Judge brought up geography and asked Proverbs whether the world was round or flat, Proverbs was silent for a moment. Then he began to nod, his head working up and down like a handle on a pump, almost as if he were pulling a reply deep out of the earth. "It don't make no matter to me," he declared. "I can teach both systems." Although Proverbs's scientific knowledge was deficient, his gumption struck me as admirable.

If you remain adaptable, you will find ways out of tight predicaments. In the year I taught in Syria, examinations took place long after classes ended. When classes concluded at the end of the second semester, Vicki and I left Syria and traveled in the Dodecanese. After six weeks we returned to Syria so I could grade examinations. In our absence visa regulations had changed, and although my passport stated that I was an employee of Tishrin University in Latakia and contained a reentry permit appropriate when we left the country, immigration refused us entry, saying we had to sail back to Cyprus and obtain a new visa. Until I lied, saying that several important members of the army would be angry if Vicki and I were denied entry, the official at the port refused to let us off the boat. Even after he allowed us off the boat, he took our passports, saying we could not leave the compound without them and that he was going to send us and the passports back to Cyprus on the evening boat. With that he departed, and Vicki and I talked our way out of the compound and went to the university. The dean of the college said "the law was the law" and refused to help us. The man, however, who would have been obliged to grade my three hundred or so examinations had we been forced out of the country, took matters into his hands. Together we visited a series of officials. Initially we had little success, but as we climbed the ladder of rank and officialdom, treatment got better. By late afternoon we were in a suite at the top of a building, the office, I was told, of the military commandant for northern Syria. While my colleague told my story, shaking his head despondently, I tried to look affable and naive. When my colleague finished the tale, the commandant made a clucking sound, then reached across his desk and made a telephone call. An hour later we were in our apartment, passports in hand.

That night my colleague brought the examinations to the apartment. When a student finished an examination, he wrote his name at the top. A black flap was then glued down over his name. Only after the registrar received the graded examination was the name revealed, thus insuring that favoritism played no part in the results. After placing the examinations on the dining room table, my colleague said that he had told the commandant that two influential generals would be pleased if Vicki and I received new visas. "Of course," he said, "I must now speak to the generals and tell them I used their names. That would be easier if I had some good news for them." From the pile of papers he removed the top two examinations, flaps still glued over the students' names. "This," he said, looking at one paper, "is the examination taken by the daughter of one general. The other is that of the niece of the second general. I have read both. Neither, I am afraid, is quite up to passing, but perhaps you could find enough points somewhere to get the girls through." When I looked startled, he added, "Use your conscience, of course, but if the girls passed, things would be easier for me." With that he got up, saying as he walked out the door, "It certainly is good to have you back. For a while I didn't think I could get you in, but then I thought of the generals."

Fifty is a passing grade in Syria. On an ordinary examination anywhere from a quarter to three-fifths of the students pass a course. I read the two papers. Both girls made thirty-five. I wasn't sure what to do. I did not believe that the papers had been written by relatives of generals. Most likely my colleague had private reasons for wanting the two students to pass; perhaps they came from his village or were kinsfolk or maybe he owed favors to their families. Whatever the reason, it had little to do with me. All I had to do was mark the papers. Before writing grades on the papers, I paused. If my integrity wasn't at risk, which it was, at the least, I thought, some educational principle was at stake. Yet as I sat in my comfortable chair in my comfortable apartment, eating a pomegranate, I understood that integrity and principle were beside the point. What mattered was that Vicki and I were not steaming toward Cyprus, perspiration running off us in rivers. "When abroad, act broadly," I thought to myself, and picking up my pen I wrote "51" across both examinations.

The day had been tiring, and I slept well that night. The next morning, though, the grades bothered me. Throughout the year and during all my years of teaching I had tried to treat students equally and fairly. I didn't want to leave Syria having acted badly. I fretted most of the morning away, but then suddenly flexibility and a simple solution came to mind. Grade inflation was rampant on American campuses. Why not import a bit of America into Syria and curve the marks so that everyone who scored thirty-five or better passed the examination? That, of course, is what I did, passing an unheard-of eighty percent of the class and feeling good about it, and myself, too.

Flexibility helps create an optimistic outlook. The flexible person knows he can probably untie knots more intricate than mazes. At times, however, optimism is so out of place that it undermines assignments and not simply the pleasures but also the seriousness of study. "You can write about anything," a teacher told Eliza in middle school, "so long as you describe a tragedy followed by a triumph." "Daddy, I want to write about the Armenian massacre in Turkey," Eliza said that night, "but how could there be a triumph if hundreds of thousands of people were slaughtered? I asked the teacher and she said that maybe someone learned a lesson and became better." "There was no triumph, only horror and damnation," I said. "No lesson was learned. Man never learns from the past. If a historian tells you we study history so that we will not repeat the mistakes of the past, you are talking to a dreamer, a person so bent on seeing a butterfly metamorphosing within the silk of tragedy that he doesn't notice that parasites have drained life from the caterpillar and reduced the cocoon to a shell." "Oh, Daddy," Eliza said, "that's too harsh." Eliza was correct. Although I was right about Armenia and the assignment, I had spoken too pessimistically to a child. Generally, though, I err on the side of optimism.

For an assignment in a class I taught on children's literature, I instructed students to write a cheerful story with a positive ending. "I am sorry I did not follow the assignment," a boy wrote on a note he handed in with his story. "But I just couldn't think of a cheerful tale. All my stories kept coming out the other way around with Evil triumphing. I am a very disobedient person by nature." I gave the boy an A. Not only did the boy's note knock common sense into my head but his story was a crackerjack.

Students' Knowledge

Every spring Slubey Garts, a minister in Carthage, traveled about Smith County, sowing salvation. One Tuesday he traveled beyond Dugget, stopping at every shack in White Lady and Devil's Bellrope. Near Guess Creek he asked an old woman if she had heard how Jesus died. "Is he dead?" the woman exclaimed. "Lord have mercy. I didn't know he was dead. I don't take no newspaper, and if you lived back in these coves, you wouldn't know much about it yourself. Tell you what I am going to do," the woman said, sucking on a pipe. "Just as soon as you leave I'm going to pray about it. I believe in letting the good Lord take care of such things." Students, I am afraid, know less about religion, indeed about almost everything, than the old woman. One of my students flew home to Atlanta this Thanksgiving. The girl had been born in Hartford but she had lived in Georgia for six years. On seeing her in class the first day after the holiday, I said, "Thank goodness you are safe. Is everybody in your family all right?" "Yes," she said, looking puzzled, "why do you ask?" "I read somewhere," I said, "that Sherman burned Atlanta. I was so worried about you that I could hardly eat any turkey much less cranberries on Thanksgiving. Did your house escape the flames?" When the girl's expression remained blank, I asked the class to explain my reference. No one could. Sherman and the Civil War were gone with the years.

You cannot take knowledge for granted. Your students will know little about the subject you teach. Instead, though, of falling into platitudinous rancor and mumbling about the decay of learning, recollect your years at school. How much did you know in sixth grade or freshman year in college? I was an ignoramus with a mind as blank as tofu. Be patient and explain carefully and students will learn, though perhaps not immediately. Knowledge like a corpse in a river sinks, then later and unexpectedly rises to the surface. Last month near Carthage a terrapin pulled himself out of a ditch and started across a dirt road. Crossing the road took the terrapin a week. Just as he pushed into grass growing on the far shoulder, a huge oak tree thumped down behind the terrapin, kicking dust over his carapace and practically obliterating his trail across the road. After wheezing and snorting for half an hour, the terrapin lowered the front lobe of his plastron and, sticking his head out, spat, then looked around. "Great God Almighty," the terrapin said on seeing the oak not more than a tail's length from the tip of his shell. "Mammy was right. It pays to be lively."

Few people are called to teaching. Most stumble into it like they stumble into marriage. Twenty years after leaping bright-eyed into the classroom, teachers glance at desks and bulletin boards and wonder how they got there, in much the same way that husbands and wives stare across the dinner table and wonder how that man or woman sitting across from them slurping ice cream got into the kitchen. Because most teachers are not called to the desk, unlike some folks to the pulpit, they are generally flexible, not thinking right and wrong absolutes.

For good teachers, people sure of themselves, rules are only guidelines, margins beyond which life thrives. Rarely is the person who slavishly follows rules a good teacher, or maybe even a decent human being. Years ago my father was foreman of a jury in Nashville. Because he did not follow legal rules, justice prevailed. A cook at the Maxwell House Hotel in Nashville made a batch of apple pies. To cool the pies the cook set them on a window ledge. Unfortunately when she was bringing the pies back inside, the cook knocked one of them off the ledge. The pie fell on the head of a woman walking along Church Street. The woman sued the Maxwell House claiming the pie damaged her brain, making it impossible for her to stop blinking. In the courtroom she blinked nonstop.

"She had the worst case of blinking imaginable," Father said. The trial began late in the morning, and the judge recessed the court for lunch. Father did not want to eat downtown, so he drove to a restaurant on Nolensville Road. "I had just started eating," Father said, "when I glanced across the dining room and saw the woman eating lunch with her lawyer. She wasn't blinking." Not once during the meal did Father see the woman blink. Father ate quickly and left the restaurant. He realized what he saw was privileged information and inadmissible in court. He knew that if he told the judge what he'd seen he would be excused from the jury. An alternate would replace him and the woman would win a big sum of money. "So I did what any decent person would do," Father said. "I kept quiet, and when the jury reconvened after lunch I spoke first." He told the jurors, "This is a clear case of neglect. The pie caused this woman to blink terribly, and I think we should award the poor soul a lot of money to prevent this kind of accident from happening again. I suggest we give her two hundred and fifty dollars." The rest of the jurors agreed with Father. "The verdict and the award," Father recounted, "cured the woman but did serious damage to her lawyer. She stared wide-eyed and he started blinking."

Do not let rules constrict your humanity. Many years ago my uncle Coleman collapsed in Houston, suffering from dementia. Although I had not seen him in twenty-nine years, I flew to Texas and took over his affairs. I sold his house and placed him in a nursing home. At a bank I set up an account entitled "Samuel Francis Pickering Agent and Attorney in fact for Coleman Enoch Pickering." Paying my uncle's bills from Storrs, then reimbursing myself, would have produced a confusing paper trail, and I established the account so the banking record would read like a primer. From a checkbook I learned that Coleman received eleven hundred dollars a month from Social Security and a pension. The checks were mailed to his house and deposited by a yard man. While in Texas, I arranged to have the checks posted to the new account.

The task was not easy. Government employees instructed me to bring Coleman to their offices and sign papers. Coleman could not get out of bed, much less wander downtown Houston.

Snags were so many and so sharp that I considered abandoning the pension and Social Security. Then I talked to two government employees, compassionate rule-benders. "Mr. Pickering," one said, "if you go by regulations, you will never be able to get your uncle's Social Security deposited in that account. Government does not exist to help people who are trying to be kind. Let me tell you what to do." The woman then suggested that I call the Social Security department in Washington and arrange for Coleman's check to be deposited directly into the account. "You will have to pretend that you are your uncle," the woman said. "The man on the phone in Washington will ask you some questions," she continued, "but here is what they are." Another understanding woman told me how to arrange for the direct deposit of Coleman's pension. "Get form 1099A from the bank," she instructed. "You will have to sign your uncle's name a couple of times. But you will just have to do that if you want to help him." "Holy cow," Vicki said when I returned from Houston. "Did school teach you to be dishonest?" "Yes, but not dishonest, decent," I said. "Helping children has taught me many good lessons."

If students miss a test, be sensible and let them take it another time. Use your judgment and don't probe too deeply to find out why the students were absent. I never force students to reveal the intimate. If you suspect something important is troubling an individual and upsetting his life, make sure he sees a counselor. Most students, though, simply sleep through my tests and mistake the days of examinations. I always prepare extra tests for such folks. One semester when I taught three hundred students, I wrote seven different examinations. Moreover, what sort of person refuses to overlook minor error? Perfection is an ideal, something, maybe, to imagine, maybe to give direction to life, but not something by which to judge flawed humans—others or ourselves.

Sad things happen to people, both children and adults. One spring semester my best student was manic-depressive. "I wish I could sit on the grass and just enjoy the season," she wrote in an essay. "I dream of being able to stroll across the campus and listen to the red-winged blackbirds in the reeds around Mirror Lake. I dream of my mind's being free to follow ripples churned yellow and blue by muskrats. Alas, whenever I walk, I cannot escape the sound of pills shaking in my backpack." During the course the girl wrote five papers and received an A on each. Unfortunately she misplaced her pills before the final examination. Instead of answering any of the questions on the examination, she rambled through two blue books, wondering why "the coffee lady" wasn't parked in her usual spot that morning. I looked at the test, then tossed it aside and gave the girl an A.

Although I don't know any device to replace exams, especially in large classes, exams distort, rewarding the glib and the quick. Usually glibness and quickness result from study and preparation. Still, exams penalize some students. Once I taught a course in poetry. Students wrote five essays and took two tests. One of my students wrote wonderful essays, crafting each thought and sentence. On both examinations she wrote a single paragraph.

She could not write quickly. Again I discounted the tests and gave her an A. Why, I wonder, should speed matter on a test like the SATs. Why shouldn't a child be allowed unlimited time to answer questions? Speed-reading has always been ludicrous; by the same token speed-testing is absurd.

No matter how you kick and rant, however, you won't change much of the system. Still, you can bend rules. If you are frightened to do so, you are probably not strong enough to teach. You are in the classroom to better the lives of children, sometimes better their lives for the future but more often in the present. The spring of his junior year my son Francis asked Martha to the junior prom. An A student who starred in school musicals, Martha suffered from sinus infections. The morning of the prom she did not go to school. She didn't miss much. Students attending the prom were released from school at eleven o'clock. After calculus class, Francis came home and napped. At three-thirty that afternoon the telephone rang, and a girl asked to speak to Francis. "He's asleep," I said. "Do you want me to wake him?" "Yes," a small voice answered. An administrator had just called Martha, informing her that because she had been absent that morning she could not attend the prom. When the administrator phoned, no one was at Martha's house to stand up for her. Her parents were divorced, and her mother worked in Hartford to support Martha and her two brothers. "Teachers exist to better children's lives," I lectured a member of the school board and then the district superintendent twenty minutes later. "Only cruel people enforce rules that bruise fragile youngsters." In talking to the superintendent, I raised the stakes. "And you know, of course, that sixteen-year-old girls suffer from feminine ailments, something I would prefer not talking about in detail now." "No, no, neither would I," the superintendent answered hastily. Ten minutes before Francis arrived at Martha's house to take her to the prom and while I sat outside the dance hall to ensure that the couple was admitted, the administrator called again. "They tell me you are a good student, and I have decided to make an exception and let you attend the dance," the administrator said.

Ignoring and finding ways around harsh rules will cause you anxiety. But at the end of your life what you will regret more than anything else will be those moments when you acted expediently and safely rather than decently. Years transform even the brightest and best of us into time servers. Responsibility for others outside the classroom becomes a burden, taking the hop and hope out of our steps. We nurse parents and offspring. We care for neighbors, and we lack the energy of youth. In *Romeo and Juliet,* Juliet asks Romeo, "Dost thou love me?" In part Romeo is a ne'er-do-well, in some respects a bum. He could have responded rudely, and Juliet risks being hurt when she asks the question. The good teacher must rise to the occasional moment and be strong enough to take risks. Doing so may cause worry, but it will also strengthen. Most of us reach the noose of our days disgruntled by the many accommodations we've made for comfort's sake, if not for money. At the conclusion of "On the Pleasure of Hating," William Hazlitt, the nineteenth-century English essayist, asked rhetorically if he had reason to despise himself. "Indeed I do," he wrote, "and chiefly for not having hated and despised the world enough." You must not hate the world. If you sink into hatred you may startle the occasional student, but you will lose most of your class. By the same token, however, you must avoid those expediencies that harm others. You must take risks not simply for students but for yourself. If you do not, you may despise yourself.

Often not acting is the best form of acting. The good educational life requires more tolerance than the good religious life. Unlike preachers, teachers are behind the pulpit five days rather than one day a week. In a good classroom many are chosen, and both the path and the gate are wide. It is easy to be a petty tyrant, mocking and scorning, especially when you are tired. For the first six weeks of classes Butch did not say a single word in freshman English. Then one day when we were starting *King Lear,* I asked, "What do Goneril and Regan think about their father?" Amazingly Butch waved his hand. "Yes, Butch," I said, beaming. "They don't give a shit about their father," Butch said.

The answer startled the class. "That is inappropriate," I thought. "I can't let a student get away with that sort of remark. If I do, I will lose control of the class." For a moment I was tempted to be harsh. I wasn't. Instead I answered, "Absolutely right, they don't give a p-p-p-p-poop about their father." The absurdity of the *p*'s popping like exhaust shifted attention from Butch to me, and students giggled. After class I called the dean of freshmen. I learned that Butch was a veteran who had spent thirteen months in hospitals and had been released only two weeks before school began. The dean was worried because Butch was silent in class. His speaking was a breakthrough for him. Did Butch graduate from college? No, he failed out after his freshman year. I am certain he has absolutely no memory of me, but I have not forgotten him. That moment in class taught me lessons. I realized that my dignity was insignificant and that often not responding to slights or violations of decorum or rule is more important than responding.

Pomposity is, incidentally, great fun if it is used playfully and does not undermine humility, creating barriers between you and other people. Be warned: children are experts at deflating the overblown. Play the fool but don't be one unintentionally, if you can help it. Years ago I found a copy of the *Carthage Courier* for May 1919. On the front page was an announcement for an All-Day Service at the Gainesboro Methodist Church. I showed the paper to Father, and he told me a story about Gainesboro, an out-of-the-way, red-clay, tarpaper town in Jackson County, Tennessee. About the only people who traveled to Gainesboro regularly were drummers, and they usually traveled by horse, staying at a small hotel run by Miss Polly Gittings. One fall day just as Miss Polly stepped out of the house onto the porch to ring the lunch bell, a drummer splashed up, his horse caked with mud. A smart aleck, he stopped in front of Miss Polly and in a silk-stocking accent tinged with high tea he said, "Madame, could you tell me where Gainesboro, Tennessee, can be found?" Miss Polly took her hand away from the bell rope and turning around looked the drummer up and down. Then as people began to gather for lunch, she said, "If you'll just jump down off your horse, you'll be up to your ass in it right now."

Although older teachers generally lack the energy of beginning teachers and responsibility may make some older teachers less inclined to stray from the fold of rule, people who have been in the classroom for decades can be more tolerant and kinder than the young. Fresh from school, minds loaded with a regimen of courses, many of which supposedly will guide them through the thickets of everyday school life, some young teachers can be narrow. A person has to age into realizing that little in life is clear. Most is shadowy. Because young lawyers have not lived long enough to understand the contingent, they make ferocious and, often, blind prosecutors.

Letter Four: Words

DEAR TEACHER,

Some years ago I read Sydney Lea's *Hunting the Whole Way Home,* a collection of essays about writing, hunting, and family. I had not seen Sydney in two decades. The last time I went hunting was with Sydney. In 1973 we hunted woodcock. He shot one bird, and I didn't shoot anything, something typical because I was a terrible shot. When Sydney wrote the book he, like me, was middle-aged. Now, when he hunted, he recounted, he pointed his shotgun but did not pull the trigger. Years had taught him control. Learning not to pull the trigger is important for the good teacher. Not pulling the trigger is difficult for me, especially when a linguistic buzzard soars overhead. In September one of my advisees came to see me. The girl's grades rose and fell like temperature in the spring, reflecting an erratic inner thermometer. "You had some difficulty last year. How are you doing now?" I asked. "I'm kicking ass this semester," the girl responded. "Oh," I said, not pulling a trigger but mentally fondling an arrow, "does that mean you are performing satisfactorily?" "You bet your ass it does," the girl said.

Changing verbal times have forced me to develop a contraceptive ear, at least in my office. In class I impose a high, out-of-date standard on speech, not something all teachers will be able to do. I impose the standard in hopes of enriching students' linguistic tastes and capacities, practically the same reason I introduce students to art, music, even furniture, things far removed from the popular MTV culture of their daily lives. With many students, high standards do not take. Last year I corrected a student's manners and language. "You need," I said, "to learn civility." The girl looked puzzled. "Civility?" she answered. "What's that? I'm not an English major."

Language is forever in flux, and if I am priggish I'm not quite hidebound. Two years ago a student asked me to recommend her for a foreign study program in London. The girl was not a creative student. I asked her to write two pages describing her life and the course she wished to study in Britain. "I feel as though by going on this excursion I will become a better teacher and person," she began, and I snoozed, despairing of writing a good letter. The girl's last two sentences woke me. "Also I wish to join a parrot club in London since I have a great passion for birds. At home we have thirty-five parrots." "Tell me about the parrots," I said to the girl after the next class. "They imitate each other," she said. "Mom and Dad argue a lot, and sometimes all the parrots start shouting 'Fuck you!' Other times they make farting sounds, and when police cars pass the house, they shriek like sirens." After describing the parrots to Vicki at dinner that night, I wrote a colorful recommendation, and the girl spent the next year in London.

Time has not loosened the girdle binding the language of all students, though. "I don't care what courses I take in English,"

Karen, my advisee, said, "as long as they don't contain smut." Against my recommendation, Karen took my course on eighteenth-century literature. After the first class, she and I reached a linguistic accommodation. Just before I strayed into bawdry, I looked at Karen and said, "Smut." She then cupped her hands over her ears. When my words wandered back to the pure and the proper I lifted my left arm, showing Karen the palm of my hand as if I were at a prayer meeting, whereupon Karen removed her hands from her ears.

What is important is that you impose some standard while simultaneously remaining flexible enough to appreciate difference and variety. You must be strong, however. Children are not adults, and you must stamp propriety on your class. Because of their lives at home or the absence thereof, the speech of some children resembles headcheese, vulgarity spotting it like fat. Do your best to improve speech. Often speech determines the future. By the by, while pondering verbal and other matters, jettison the word *precedent*. *Precedent* is heavy as an anchor and drowns more good ideas than any other word I know. It is a "thou shalt not" word cloaked in black seriousness. Under the guise of intellectuality it murders.

Recess

Early in my career a student told me a story. Three anthropologists from New Jersey, he said, went to the Amazon to search for a lost tribe. Unfortunately the tribe found them before they found it and, binding their hands and tying them neck to neck, tribe members led them back to their village. Each of the anthropologists was then bound to a stake and sticks were piled around his feet, after which the village chief, dressed in toucan feathers and assorted bones, approached. Stopping before the first anthropologist the chief said, "Which do you prefer: death or bunga, bunga?" Understandably the anthropologist answered, "Bunga, bunga." This caused great joy in the village, and the natives began to dance, shouting "bunga, bunga" and shaking huge orange gourds. When the initial enthusiasm died down, two natives came forward, untied the anthropologist, and led him to the riverbank, where they chopped off his tits and testicles and put caterpillars in his ears, ants up his nose, and leeches in his navel. Then they dragged him back to the stake and amid peals of good-natured laughter burned him alive.

After the commotion subsided and the smoke blew away, the chief approached the second anthropologist and said, "Which do you prefer: death or bunga, bunga?" The second anthropologist didn't know what to say. For a moment he thought about choosing death, but hope springs eternal, even beside the Amazon, and convincing himself that the chief must have misunderstood his colleague when he asked for bunga, bunga instead of death, he said in a loud, clear voice, "Bunga, bunga." Almost immediately two natives ran forward, tore him from the stake, and dragged him to the river where they served him much as they did his companion, after which they reduced him to charcoal. Having seen what happened to his friends, the third anthropologist was ready for the chief and when asked whether he preferred death or bunga, bunga he said, "Death." For a moment a pall fell over the village; the natives dropped their gourds, and the chief turned away from the anthropologist, shoulders sagging and toucan feathers drooping. The gloom did not last long, however. Suddenly the chief smiled, squared his shoulders, and turning back to the anthropologist said, "Death you have asked for. Death you shall have." Then raising his voice and waving his gourd, he added, "But first a little bunga, bunga."

What, you wonder, does that story have to do with teaching? The answer is nothing. Indeed I want the story to undercut the seriousness with which you take this book. Read the book. Ponder some things then push it aside and move beyond it. Advice is suggestion. At its most valuable advice is a catalyst for analysis and thought. Rarely should you follow it slavishly. What one person does easily and effectively may not suit you. By all means ask your colleagues for advice. Listen and learn. One of the ways you will learn is by differing with them. Don't simply mimic their actions. Only one cloud really darkens my teaching, and that cloud blew across my first year at Dartmouth. One day early in May I walked across the green in Hanover. Spring had finally come and the lawn was crowded with people. Blue jeans had melted away and girls blossomed like crocus, yellow and purple, aglow with smiles and hope. No one seemed in a hurry, and people milled about absorbing the milky promises of the season. Suddenly the mood was broken. A student came out of a building and, seeing someone across the green he knew, yelled, "Fuck you!" The cry bounced back and forth off buildings, and by the time the echo died spring had faded. Before realizing it, I crossed the green and stopped the boy. I was too angry to say anything sensible, so I told him to be in my office the next morning at eight o'clock.

Walking back to the English Department, I wondered what I would say the next day. By then a lecture on manners would strike the student, and me, as pompous. At a loss, I went to an older, distinguished, and supposedly shrewd colleague for advice. "This is easily taken care of," he said, and then described what he had once done. Something about what he did jarred me, but since he was more experienced and I could think of nothing else to do, I suppressed doubt and followed his suggestion. The next morning when the student appeared in my office I told him to sit down. Then I turned away and began grading papers. I heard my clock ticking, and time inched by, each second seeming an age. Finally the student burst out, "Aren't you going to say anything?" I turned around slowly, stared at him, and said, "Get out." "What?" he said. "Get out," I repeated. "You aren't worth talking to." He got up, started to speak, but then slumped out silently. For a moment I felt exhilarated. The feeling, though, like spring on the green, quickly passed, and ever since I have felt small and guilty. Never again have I followed a colleague's advice without mulling it over and over. What I did was cruel. I stripped the boy of dignity and self-respect and, if he resembles me, gave him a recollection that will always make him cringe.

In urging you to handle advice as carefully as you would a porcupine, I do not want you to undervalue the importance of the people with whom you teach. Students come and go. In comparison faculties are constant. You may teach with the same people for thirty years. Members of the faculty will become your friends. If someone dislikes you, chances are that he will be a person with whom you teach. Don't hold grudges, and forget slights. Not only may the person who slights you yesterday become your friend tomorrow, but some slights are actually funny. "Sam," a colleague once said to me, "you hide your learning better than anyone I have ever met." Words, as the old saying puts it, are nice but chickens lay eggs. Deeds, not words, matter, although words are a species of deed. What bothers me, and this is one of my favorite hobbyhorses, is that often words pass for deeds. Instead of to the person who does the heavy lifting, people often give credit to the person who groans. On the wall of the Travelers' Aid office in the old Providence bus station was once a big orange poster, black letters proclaiming, "Consider Yourself Hugged." Instead of embracing some of the sad people who stumbled through the station, it was more sanitary, and probably safer, to keep them a few syllables away at sentence length, wrapping them about with words, not arms.

Nevertheless, words are in a sense Lego blocks. If you use words well, you can sometimes determine how people see events, that is, you can construct reality. By doing so, you can both make life easier and make life itself. One Sunday my son Francis took two showers, one at ten in the morning and the other at nine in the evening. "Do you realize," I said, opening the bathroom door and addressing Francis while he was in the shower, "that this is the second shower you have had today?" "No," Francis said. "I took only one shower today. This is tomorrow's shower." In describing a preacher, Loppie Groat, one of my Carthage characters, said, "His talk is so melodious that dead folks sit up in coffins and put on hearing aids just to listen to him." "But wouldn't the corpses bump their heads when they sat up?" Eliza said, not being swept away by my words.

In any case at the same time that using words well can oil daily life, it can also become addictive and corrupting. You must lift and help your colleagues with more than talk. For example if your school system is not unionized, it should be. Pitch in and help organize. Health benefits are important, more so than salary. Get to know your fellow teachers well. Discover their interests and ask about their families and dreams. You should know your colleagues well enough to sense sadness and happiness. You must also know them well enough to criticize, particularly when faculty treat students badly. "The teacher caught me smoking two blocks away from school, ten feet short of the border that separated school from town. He told me to come to his office the next morning," Chris recounted. "I asked him not to call my mother, explaining she had just learned my grandfather was dying from lung cancer and was very fragile. I don't think he intended to call my parents, at least not until he discovered he could cause unhappiness. When I told him about my grandfather, the man chuckled and immediately picked up the phone. He laughed when Mother cried." Horsewhipping is out of favor. Verbal lashing remains a punishment, one of last resort, for it may make an enemy, but it is something that you may have to use on a colleague once or twice during your career.

As a teacher, your responsibility extends beyond the classroom. Your life is more public than, say, that of a banker. Escaping into privacy and irresponsibility is difficult. Whatever you do has the potential to influence someone else's child. If you smoke, you should stop. I preach and urge. I tell students that I do not give good grades to fools, and that anyone who smokes, jaywalks, or rides a bicycle without a helmet cannot make higher than a C in my class. When I see my students smoking, I don't call their parents but I do urge them to stop. I have bought students bicycle helmets. Of course I don't lower grades for dangerous behavior. Occasionally, though, at the end of a blue book, I will write a note saying, "This paper is worth an A. But I do not give high grades to nitwits, and since you smoke, I have given you a C-." I always draw an arrow from the note pointing to the next page on which I give the student the mark he made. Last year a student didn't notice the arrow. "You can't do this," she said. "I made an A." "I did do it," I said. "You should be reported," she said. "Go ahead and do so," I said. "Hordes of people have reported me for dreadful things, and I'm still here." Shortly afterward the girl noticed the arrow. Did she stop smoking? No. She tried but failed. "I'm going to stop someday," she said at graduation. "I'm not going to be smoking at twenty-five." "Good," I said.

Every spring Vicki and I put on Wellingtons and clean the creek running from the spillway under Mirror Lake in the middle of the campus to Route 195. We like being outside and wearing boots. Cleaning makes me feel better about myself and for a moment deludes me into thinking I can tidy life. In part, though, I clean in the fond but probably silly hope that students will see me. Later maybe they will remember the sight of me at work and as a result will themselves be more apt to sweep and scrub. On New Year's Eve Vicki and I collected garbage from the Nipmuck Trail, from Gurleyville Road through the Ogushwitz Meadow. We harvested hundreds of beer cans and enough plastic to shrink-wrap our house five times over. No student saw us, but a man stopped and asked what we were doing. When I told him, he said, "That's really good." Then he stopped, his brow furrowing as he searched for words. "You must be . . ." he continued, pausing again. "You must be a socialist." On coming home, Vicki fed the dogs, and I opened champagne, the hearty $9.99-a-bottle variety. "Well done," I said as we celebrated the new year.

The community in which you teach will become important to you. Teachers, at least English teachers, don't retire because classes become onerous. Grading papers drives them from school. Most teachers miss students. Even more than students, they miss the friends of lunch and office. "I can't retire," my friend Ray told me two years ago. "I would miss you people too much." If I retired, I think my emotions would dry, and I'd shrivel. Every day I go to the English Department and join friends while they eat lunch. I am a nibbler, so I don't eat. I simply want to visit people whom I have grown to love. If you are lucky you will understand. My friend Roger is quick and sometimes caustic, his favorite expression being, "So what's your point?" One day last April when I had gotten up at 3:30 A.M. to grade papers and was exhausted beyond restraint, one of Roger's remarks so irritated me that I stood and shouted "Fuck you" at him. "Actually eight F-you's," Tom said later. After whacking the words home I stalked out of the lunchroom and went to my office, flopping into the chair behind my desk. I did not stay in the office long. "What have I done?" I thought. "Life without these friends would be barren." I raced back to the lunchroom and bursting through the door said, "I think I misspoke myself."

For some people saying "I'm sorry" is difficult. In this life, however, only hermits don't have to say "I was wrong." As a teacher escaping the presence of others is difficult, and you will err many times and have to apologize. Learning to say "I'm sorry" will be important not only for you but for your students. If your students become self-aware enough that they learn to apologize, you will have taught them an important lesson.

Curiosity

Good teachers are curious. They are rummagers and explorers. Curiosity enriches life. The curious teacher seizes days and in the process usually broadens sympathies and understanding. As interests grow, so does contentment. Instead of moping through hours, the curious person escapes self and rancorous moodiness. Instead of murdering to dissect, the good teacher dissects in order to appreciate. Curiosity nurtures capacious appreciation. In the early nineties my children attended school in Australia for a year. Rarely was the year less than marvelous. One day in December classes were canceled at Eliza's school for the "pet show." Children brought a zoo of creatures to school: guinea pigs named Winkle and Bubble; cats named Smoky, Ophelia, and Princeton; budgies called Blueberry, Cheep-Cheep, Feathers, and Max; and rabbits named Oops, Benjamin, Peewee, Goldy, and Long Tail. A local butcher presented a marrow bone to the dog with "the waggiest tail." A poodle wearing the bottom of a battered tutu won the contest for best-dressed dog, taking home a necklace made from dog biscuits. Other dogs did or tried to do tricks. A little girl pushed a moplike puppy around in a stroller. When a boy blew his harmonica, a golden retriever sat on his haunches and looked happy. Only after the boy nudged him with his foot did the dog wag his tail.

A woman from the Department of Conservation and Land Management brought two orphans to school: a fourteen-month-old echidna and a fifteen-month-old kangaroo. I held both of them, the kangaroo like a baby, my arms wrapped around and under its back, the echidna swathed in a thick towel. The echidna's back resembled a thicket planted to deter wayward boys from taking shortcuts through a yard. Soft and hairy, the animal's belly rolled like Christmas pudding. A parent sat on a stone wall holding a nervous mutt. She had gotten the dog from the pound four days earlier. "I believe in recycled clothes and animals," she said. "The dog already knows I am her mistress. In the old days, stockmen," she explained, "forced dogs' jaws open and spat down their throats. That's how they imprinted themselves on the dogs. I did the same thing. Only I did it in a ladylike way. I spat in my palm and put my hand in front of the dog's muzzle. She licked the spittle off, and now she knows me. If you ever get a dog from the pound, spit in your hand and make her lick it, and you won't have any trouble training her."

The day was almost perfect, blemished only by a thoughtless teacher, one with a limited capacity for appreciation. Edward and Eliza did not exhibit pets. Edward's black house spider was dangerous, and he knew he couldn't take it to school. Eliza, though, wanted to show Albert, the big Australian cockroach I'd caught for her. But when she asked her teacher if she could bring Albert to school, the woman grimaced and said, "Ugh, how awful. Don't bring that ugly thing here." In truth Albert was beautiful, resembling a long black bullet. The next term Eliza had a different teacher, a glorious woman who encouraged her to appreciate life's great gifts, many of them as small as Albert but still great.

The pleasures of curiosity are limitless. One September I attended a Municipal Inland Wetland Commissioners Training Program, sponsored by the Connecticut Department of Environmental Protection. I went to the program to listen to discussions of hardpan and to learn to read maps. I wanted to know differences between soils: Leicester, Ridgeway, Wilbraham, Rumney, Walpole, and Whitman. I wanted to progress beyond books to reading the earth, to know that yellow soils are usually aerated and well drained while gray soils often lack oxygen and are saturated with water. Participants in the program received a broadside of "Soil Facts," published by the National Wildlife Federation. Most of the facts were simple statements such as "Roots hold soil together and help prevent erosion." Some startled me, however. Spread over an acre, five tons of topsoil supposedly creates a layer of new dirt no thicker than a dime. Although that statement made me pause, what forced me to resuscitate high school mathematics was the assertion that "one earthworm can digest 36 tons of soil in one year." Thirty-six tons, I wrote the National Wildlife Federation, is seventy-two thousand pounds. To digest that much dirt a worm would have to munch through 197.26 pounds of soil a day or slightly more than 8.2 pounds an hour, three hundred and sixty-five days a year, with no time off for cold weather, rest, sex, or to avoid robins or rain. "Only one big mother of a worm could eat that much dirt," I wrote, "one that had been raised on chemicals. My advice to someone who found such a worm down amongst his crabgrass would be," I said, "to take his leg in his hand and heist himself out of there and head down the road as fast as he could." "Oops, maybe 36 pounds a year, but I even doubt that," a man wrote back from the National Wildlife Federation. "What is astonishing is that you are the first person to question the statistic."

Interests

"Our great and glorious masterpiece is to live appropriately," Montaigne wrote. The problem is that people disagree over what is appropriate, particularly over what is appropriate for folks other than themselves. School and life are to a great extent what you make of them. Often, though, you can shape not simply what is appropriate but happiness and success as well. Not long after Samp Griggs moved to Carthage and opened an accountant's office, he got a sty on his eyelid and went to Dr. Sollows. "Now Sollows," he said, after the sty had been lanced, "what sort of people live in this burg?" "You have just come here from Lebanon," Dr. Sollows answered, "what were folks like there?" "Scoundrels all, even the children," Griggs said, shaking his head, "mean, suspicious, you name it." "Oh," Dr. Sollows said, "I am afraid you will find people here the same." Later that afternoon Jeb Buchanan visited Dr. Sollows to have a sore throat swabbed. Like Griggs, Buchanan was new to Carthage, recently having started a small soap and candle manufacturing business on Spring Street. "Dr. Sollows," he said. "Carthage has been your home for over fifty years. What are people hereabouts like?" "Well," Dr. Sollows replied, "you've come from Crossville. What did you think of people there?" "Goodness me, I hated to leave them," Buchanan answered. "They were the best folks in the world—always friendly and kind—real neighbors." "Don't worry," Dr. Sollows said smiling, "don't worry, you will find the same folks here."

Unlike a recipe for devil's food cake, that for a teacher varies, although being mischievous, albeit not satanic, may be part of it. Because it helps students and teachers escape corroding self, enthusiasm borders on the moral. The enthusiastic person refuses to be corralled and tamed to bit and convention. Enthusiasm is more alluring than beauty. Although some students invariably mock, most students respond to and respect enthusiasm. Students want to believe that life is earnest and not empty. What a person knows often determines what he sees and what he appreciates. Good teachers do not let themselves become that partial creature, their occupation. Moreover don't let time turn you into those middle-aged people who are not happy unless they are angry about something.

To educate for the future, one must educate for the moment. Classes should sprawl beyond particular subjects. In digressions lie lessons. Expose students to possibilities. Let them know about your fondness for china, birds, tag sales, and gardening. Talk to them about economics and sociology, to be sure, but also talk to them about places you have been and things you have seen and thought. Instill the awareness that for the interested person days and nights glitter. Your words don't have to transport students over the hills and far away, though occasionally they may. In our mobile society, the institution of school becomes place. Parents and children move about, but school remains a constant, sometimes practically the only constant in a child's life. Work to prevent place from becoming a prison. Encourage students to appreciate the local and the immediate, that is, their community, not simply of people but of, say, flora and fauna. You may find slipping the lead of particular lessons difficult as you must not neglect requirement and credential. Moreover you may not be constitutionally disposed toward wandering. "The people teaching you," I tell my students, "are the most conservative people in the nation. We may vote liberal, but we live conservatively. We were the boys and girls who did not disrupt or question. We handed our papers in on time. We were the children who made A's in first grade, in sixth grade, in high school, and in college. We are the people who purchase fuel-efficient cars and save money for old age. We don't live beyond our expense accounts, be those accounts emotional or financial or sometimes imaginative."

Pod Malone was the worst stutterer in Smith County. One evening after a meeting of the Knights of Pythias, Dr. Sollows, who had just read about a treatment for stutterers at Vanderbilt Hospital in Nashville, met Pod outside Read's drugstore. "Pod," he said, "have you ever attended a clinic for stutterers?" "No," Pod answered, after pulling his left ear and thinking a bit. "I just pi-pi-picked it up on my own." Class should be a place where students learn about subjects but where they also pick up things, interests and knowledge that may awaken tomorrow or years later. During the past year I have brought a miscellany of things to my literature classes: the first edition of William Thackeray's novel *The Virginian,* published in twenty monthly parts; a depiction of the Rainbow Serpent painted by an Aborigine in Arnhem Land; a Bedouin coffeepot tall as my thigh, the spout resembling the beak of a vulture; Rose Medallion plates; the head of a loon; owl pellets; and table settings of knives, forks, and spoons. Students also bring things to class to show me. One month when writing and thought were not flowing easily, Tanya brought her pet ferret

Sabine to a lecture. At the end of class Tanya set Sabine on my shoulder. For a while Sabine twisted over my back and around my neck. Abruptly, though, she stopped and, perching on my collarbone, leaned forward, dug her claws into my shoulder, and urinated down my back. "Oh, Professor," Tanya said, blushing, "Sabine has never done anything like this before. She has never peed on anyone, and I don't know why she did it now." For me, show-and-tell became show-and-write. "Tanya," I said, stepping out of the puddle at my feet and unbuttoning my shirt, all the while composing a paragraph, "this is wonderful. Now I have something to write about."

Although teachers must plan classes diligently—indeed genius may be diligence—the teaching life is messy. You don't sit in a study surrounded by leather-bound books, titles stamped on their spines in gilt. You sit in a classroom, students and their lives chaotic about you, emotions slipping loose like pages from paperbacks. Recently I saw a sheet of paper taped to a door. Marching across the paper were several lines of capital letters. "DO NOT," the letters commanded, "PLACE PAPERS UNDER THE DOOR AS THEY BECOME FILTHY AND DAMAGED. ALSO, I DO NOT WANT TO SLIP AND FALL AS A RESULT OF STEPPING ON ONE. RATHER PLACE THEM IN MY MAILBOX IN THE FACULTY MAILROOM NEXT TO THE ELEVATOR." Beware of neatening vitality out of life and students. In fact studied or planned clutter should fill the schoolroom: posters, mobiles, pictures, plants, knickknacks, and memorabilia of all sorts, and, depending on the grade, aquariums in which creatures swim and crawl, dig and burrow. Helping children, teaching them, will sometimes force you, as the maxim puts it, to fill the teakettle at the horse trough.

You will often be misunderstood. Only folks sleeping in wooden kimonos escape misunderstanding, and if biographers shovel them up, those people don't escape. You will be misquoted, and your words will be distorted. Not just strangers but even your friends will judge you by what you did not say or do. People will give credence not to what you did or meant to do but to what someone said you did. The best you can do is gird your feelings and get on with living. Time brings forgetfulness and less frequently correction. You can attempt to correct misapprehensions. Occasionally you will succeed; oftentimes, however, in calling attention to mistakes you only reinforce errors in other people's minds. An ancient rude maxim describes the problem of trying to correct the slanderous. "He who wrestleth with a turd shall be beshit, fall he under or over." Also you should not forget that people are rarely as interested in you as in themselves. What they think you did might titillate an hour but not much more. One afternoon shortly after my family and I returned to Storrs from spending twelve months in Australia, I saw a member of my English Department in the university locker room. "Sam," the person said, "you've just finished a sabbatical, haven't you? Did you go anywhere or did you stay in Storrs?"

Sometimes, however, mistakes will make you wince for months, or years. One fall a decade ago a young writer attended a class I taught in creative writing in order to gather material for a magazine article. During the class I talked about shaping believable characters. My students seemed almost unaware of human failing and the mixed nature of being. As a result they created flat characters and wrote dull, unconvincing stories. People, I pointed out conventionally enough, were complex mixtures of strengths and weaknesses. Even the best people, I said, were weak. As an illustration I sketched a fictional character for them, a decent person but a man vicariously addicted to the sensational. After every airplane crash he read the list of victims. He hoped to find the name of someone he knew, not because he wished anyone harm, for in his daily life he was gentle and kind, but simply because he was bored and wanted to feel part of an event. Imagine how he reacted, I said, when he discovered that a friend was on the plane that crashed at Lockerbie, Scotland. For hours after the crash, he called mutual acquaintances, telling them about the death of their friend.

Students grasped the point I tried to make about human nature, and for the next class several wrote stories containing deeper, richer characters. Unfortunately, the writer got things wrong. He confused me with the fictional character I created and in his article stated that I called people after the crash, experiencing "an extraordinary pleasure conveying bad news." When I saw the article I slumped over. I was a parent, and reading about the students on the plane had been almost unbearable. At bedtime the night of the crash I had squeezed my children tight against my chest, as if by pulling them close and wrapping my arms around them I could protect them against the horrors of life. "God," Vicki said on seeing the article, "what are you going to do?" "Nothing," I said, "just endure the mistake. It's not important." "Aren't you going to demand a correction?" Vicki said. "No," I said. Ten days later the writer called and asked how I liked his piece. "I liked it a lot," I said.

You will not escape mistakes. Indeed, according to a Scottish story, a ruinous mistake led to Adam and Eve's being expelled from Eden. While the Archangel Michael spoke English, Adam and Eve, the tale relates, spoke Gaelic. After Adam and Eve ate the apple, God decided to forgive them and He sent Michael to Eden to inform them. Unhappily Michael's voice roared like a cataract. Moreover he carried a flaming sword in his right hand as an emblem of justice tempered by mercy. The side of the sword that faced outward burned red hot, while the underside was cool and blue. Unable to understand English, Adam and Eve misunderstood Michael. His deep voice terrified them, and when flames from the sword flared over their heads they bolted through the Eastern Gate of Paradise and like noxious worms burrowed out of sight deep in the Wilderness. For His part God misinterpreted their actions. Thinking they had scorned His mercy, He cursed their loins, letting a lazar-like host of ailments rain down upon their offspring: "spasms, convulsions, epilepsies, fierce catarrhs, moping melancholies, and silent pestilence swinging a blood scythe."

To live appropriately is a struggle. One of the best things you can do amid the mess of class is interest students in the particular, matters close to hand that at first seem small but may enrich life more than things generally thought major or important. Small things have brought me more pleasure than great, not, I should add, that I have experienced any of the conventional greats. Indeed for teachers the real greats are domestic and take place within family, the nuclear family at home and the greater family at school. One year I wrote a short appreciation of the dandelion. Almost immediately I received bundles of mail, and my life bloomed, not like a hothouse forced by ambition but like a pasture buttery with yellow.

An eighty-nine-year-old woman sent me her picture and wrote that when she had gone to Niagara Falls on her honeymoon in 1917, dandelions were blooming. "When our three children were growing," she recounted, "they heard their dad and me say it was truly a beautiful sight and they began bringing us bouquets. Now my grandchildren and young great-grandchildren do the same every spring. This has become a tradition of love and for me the lowly and beautiful dandelion has become a glorified flower." A man in Missouri sent me a song he wrote in honor of the dandelion, while several people sent poems. A woman in Arizona sent poems on various subjects; in the fifth grade she had written about the stars. "If stars are really like the windows of Heaven, / Why are they small like a pin? / And why are the Angels allowed to peek out, / And we're not allowed to peek in?" "Your article," a woman wrote from Michigan, "sent my mind back about sixty-eight years. My older sister had brought measles home from school and passed them around to her younger sisters. When we were recovering from the measles, our yard was covered with yellow blossoms. They were the most beautiful things I had ever seen. We wanted to go outside and pick them, but our mother would not let us go outside yet. I'm seventy-two years old now and still think of the memories each spring when the lawn turns yellow. Last fall," she continued, "my home of forty-four years burned down. All I had left was the clothes I had on when I left home. My family cut logs (homegrown) and had them sawn. Now rising out of ashes and rubble is a very pretty log house. Next spring I plan to look out of the windows of my new home and enjoy the dandelions." From little seeds enjoyment blows wonderful, as colorful and as fresh as a field of wildflowers.

Letter Five: Interests

DEAR TEACHER,

If you have trouble interesting students in matters both in and without the classroom, then you probably need to roam a little and discover new interests or breathe vitality into old. Explore books and places. The places don't have to be exotic. I think I could walk Storrs's woods and meadows blindfolded. I have also wandered over a ridge or two. From travels I bring back experiences that affect my classes, usually indirectly. Although age often makes a person more tolerant, in part because doings that used to bother him no longer seem significant, age can make one short with others. On trips I frequently see or hear things that make me aware of the sadness of life and reinforce the conviction that good teaching soothes as well as educates.

Some years ago I sat in the international terminal at Logan Airport in Boston. As I ate a chocolate croissant, a mother and her little girl, two and a half or three years old, sat beside me. The girl ate a butter pecan ice-cream cone. When the ice cream melted and ran down her chin, I wiped her face with a napkin. The woman was an American living in London. Two months earlier her husband had died suddenly, and sadly she recounted that she did not think she could afford to continue living abroad. While we talked, the woman's flight was called. Getting up, she took her daughter's arm and started toward the gate. Six or so feet away from the table at which I sat, the little girl pulled loose and turning back stared at me with a puzzled expression on her face. Slowly she extended her hand toward me, her small, round fingers opening like petals in sunlight. "Daddy?" she said softly, both a question and a catch in her voice. "Daddy?"

Before putting my uncle in a nursing home, I cleaned his house. His wife Amanda had died some years earlier. She had been an elementary school teacher for three decades. In the house I found a chest packed with stacks of notes from her students. "Dear Mrs. Pickering," Kathy wrote in 1969. "You are the sweetest teacher in the whole school. You have done so many things for us, and you do everything right. I love you more than any teacher in the whole wide world." "I wish you were my teacher all through school," Claire wrote, adding, "P.S. I mean everything I've said." Tina did not want summer vacation to begin, writing, "I wish we had three more months left." "I loved being in your room," Julie wrote. "In third grade I wanted to be in it so much. You have made me feel so good with all the things you taught me in fourth grade." "You are the nicest teacher I ever had and I don't blame you for getting mad at me," Roger said. "People told me when I was in third grade that you were very hard. They said to hope that I don't get you," Debby wrote. "Now I'm glad that I got you. You have taught me more than what I'm supposed to know in fourth grade."

In 1966 Bill and his family moved to Australia, and he wrote asking for Amanda's "awdress." "I will miss you very much and

I will still write to you," he said. "You have teach me very much about oldthing long ago people and some other things. Could you come onday to see me in Australia? I will miss you if you don't." Laura drew a border of pink tulips and blue and orange daisies around her note. "You have been so nice to me," she wrote. "I love you. I have tried to be a good student this year. I hope you appreciate me." "To a GREAT teacher," Chris wrote on the envelope containing his note, adding, "From the Smartest kid in class (dumest)." "Dear Mrs. Pickering," Grace wrote. "I have enjoyed being one of your daughters, and I tried to please you. But the future years have yet to come when I will be a teacher too." Cheryl made a card from a piece of waxed cardboard, nine inches long and six and a half inches wide, sliced from the bottom of a flat box of cookies. On the card, gold and silver sprinkles swirled through blue paint. Inside Cheryl pasted cardboard letters spelling "I Love You," the first letter of each word green, the other letters yellow.

"Thank you for the frog," Scott wrote at the conclusion of his letter, "and please come over and swim sometime and visit him." Amanda's room was a menagerie, just the way I wish rooms had been when I was in elementary school. In the chest I found issues of *The Raven,* the school newspaper. "Our pet turtle which Chris Calloway brought to our room has escaped from his home on the Science table. If anyone sees a stray turtle please return him to Classroom 2," a correspondent reported from Amanda's third grade in 1947. In 1949 Snappy, a chameleon, escaped from Amanda's room. "He was tame," the reporter recounted, "but one day decided to leave. We think he became jealous of our other pets and decided to climb out the window. We hope he has found a winter home under the building." Amanda's room was quick with butterflies, grasshoppers, goldfish, ants, caterpillars, frogs, and a snake. The doings of the creatures were exciting, and the children did not mourn Snappy's loss. "One of our happiest moments," the reporter noted at the end of his article, "came when we discovered six baby snails in our bowl of thirteen tropical fish. The mother snail now has plenty of company and helpers to keep the aquarium clean."

Before school started each fall, Amanda wrote members of her last class. "Now that vacation ends and we must think of school again," she wrote, "I think once more of our little class of last year. To you, as a member of that group, I want to express my sincere appreciation for your kindness and thoughtfulness toward me as we worked together. As you continue through life, I shall derive much pleasure in feeling that I have contributed in part to each achievement of yours. That is a teacher's reward." The small letters students scrawled awkwardly across pages made me both melancholy and happy, somehow happier than the letters I receive, something I cannot explain. Maybe letters from young children smack less of craft than those written by adults. Then, too, the odd errors make such letters seem less platitudinous and thus sincerer. In any case the person who imagines he can explain everything won't be a good teacher. Oddly, when unsure of a topic, I sometimes teach better than when I know a topic thoroughly. Instead of answers jumping quickly to the tongue, I pause, and while I ponder, students have the leisure to shape thoughts. I copied excerpts from Amanda's letters into a notebook. Then I stuffed the contents of the chest into black plastic bags and, carrying them outside, set them by the end of the driveway for the trash man.

Outside

In *Tom Brown's School Days,* Thomas Hughes preached that what a child learned outside the classroom was more important than what happened inside. Tom's father, Squire Hughes, said he was not sending his son to school in order to become a scholar but "a brave, helpful, truth-telling Englishman, and a gentleman, and a Christian," albeit this last was a muscular Christian, for whom deeds not doctrine mattered. Times have changed. In some circles the word *gentleman* smacks of inbred elitism; in other circles people believe religions disrupt by dividing communities and fomenting zeal. Still, what occurs beyond school can be formative. Despite society's belief that school education shapes adults, students spend more time outside of school than inside. Although you cannot control what children do once school is over, you can influence their activities. Not only can you awaken interests but you can instill the hankering to appreciate. You can also suggest activities and steer students toward Model United Nations, debate, ballroom dance, the math club, drama, band, or the environmental club, among others. Many of your students will work after school. Showing an interest in their jobs takes little effort, a question or two. For many students what is important is protection, simply being separated from the environments in which they live. For such students, the longer the school day lasts the better. Try to find activities that interest them, then do your best to see that they get home safely. For still other students home may be dangerous. Talk to counselors. Learn what social services are available. Work hard and hope for the best. You can help individuals; not always, but sometimes. And occasionally if teachers act together they can shame society into reform.

Still other students will play athletics. Although all teachers at some time during their classroom years will be faculty advisers for sundry clubs, a few of you will coach. Thomas Hughes compared struggles on the athletic field to warfare, a metaphor that distorts sport and war, trivializing the horror of the latter and elevating the former beyond fun and high spirits. Hughes believed that boys became men on playing fields, much as they did in the far Crimea. To some degree society still believes that lessons learned in athletics may be more important than those learned in class. Once upon a time colleges celebrated the well-rounded student, the child who played *and* studied. Now admissions officers say they want a well-rounded student body. Instead of the genteel amateur able to do a lot of things adequately, colleges want experts and devotees: a French horn player, a champion debater, a quarterback, a center for the girls' basketball team. For my part I am not sure what lessons athletics teach. "I learned to cheat," a student told me. "All that inspirational stuff is crap."

Like many students, the boy overstated. Like all activities sports can be important, particularly for children in elementary and high school. If you coach, your duties extend far beyond winning. On the athletic field as in the classroom, the good coach plays all the students, the boy who can't do math and the girl who can't catch a ball but who tries and tries. I was a terrible athlete but I played many sports. The most important lesson I learned was that I was not going to be the best or number one in anything. As a result little things satisfied me, getting into a game for three plays, and since little things compose our lives I have been remarkably happy. Sports taught me to enjoy the small for what they were and not to fret. I learned that winning didn't matter as much as playing. Of course I learned other lessons. Most coaches, for example, seemed to have failed math. When they discussed giving 110 percent effort, I always wanted to point out the impossibility of such a thing.

What you should do as a coach is provide kids with happy memories. Help them make friends. Help them be better than they are, and that means you should set a good example, in word and in deed. Never forget that sports like studies should be enjoyable. The year I taught at Montgomery Bell Academy I helped coach freshman football. Practice was fun, so much so that children raced out of school to put on their gear. We tried to play every child in every game, no matter the score. During college summers I worked at a boys' camp in Maine. One summer I coached a twelve-and-under baseball team. The team was part of a camp league. Eighteen players were on the team. Nine were good athletes, and nine were terrible. If I had played my nine best athletes, the team would have won the league. I didn't. Instead I divided the boys into two squads, five good athletes on one squad, four on the other. Each squad played half of every game. The boys didn't win the league but they enjoyed themselves and grew comfortable with one another and their differences in ability. The poor athletes didn't envy the good athletes so much by summer's end, and the good athletes did not look down upon the poor athletes.

Resisting the hype surrounding sports is difficult, and despite my delightful lack of success on playing fields I pushed my children into boats and onto courts. Learning from an inner child is anatomically impossible. In contrast every parent learns from real children. One day after flying back from Houston having seen Uncle Coleman, I hurried to Spring Hill to watch Eliza play soccer. She was on a sixth-grade team. I arrived near the end of the game. Eliza was the sweeper. I did not know she had played the whole game and was tired. When she remained close to her goal while her team pushed up the field, I urged her to pick up the pace. Eliza stopped in mid-stride and, turning toward me, put her hands on her hips and shouted, "Mr. Pickering, the coach is on the other side of the field. She is a she, not a he or a you."

My thoughts about the importance of athletics are mixed. For years I have criticized big-time athletic programs at universities, thinking they both minimized learning and taught the wrong thing, that is, winning no matter the ethical costs. In truth sports are popular because they are trivial. Because so much on the front pages of newspapers is sad and disturbing, readers turn to sports pages and like blind Samson pull the columns down, burying themselves in anecdote and statistic in hope of deadening thought and sometimes conscience. Problems facing the world are so complex that they seem not only to defy solution but also to lie beyond man's abilities to cope. On the sports page life appears clearer. The quick win races, and the hardworking occasionally triumph. High schools are not universities, however, at least not yet. If you coach, don't model your program on one at a university; instead, study your class. Then transform the field into an extension of the classroom.

For me sports brought pleasure and friendship and, I am afraid, much laughter. In Cambridge the summer bumping races were the highlight of the rowing year. All colleges filled the boats, some of the larger colleges filling eight or nine. The boats raced in divisions, and a boat's position within a division depended upon the previous year's finish. Thus the second boat from St. Catharine's, my college, would start where St. Catharine's number two finished the summer before, although an entirely different group of boys composed the crew. For a race itself, a division rowed down the Cam to a lock where the boats turned about and lined up along the bank with slightly over a length of water between each shell. When a cannon was fired, each crew tried to overtake and bump the boat ahead before being bumped by the boat behind. If the two boats immediately ahead were involved in a bump, the following boat rowed by in pursuit of the boat still farther ahead.

The start was tense, and to loosen us up I always told the story of P. M. Coatsworth Wallingford, who rose to glory behind his oar, stroking Cat's to Head of the River (the first boat in Division One). Although Coats died at Haling Way, just before the Long Reach, he didn't stop rowing. All heart, he even raised the tempo to thirty-eight strokes per minute near Ditton Meadows, eventually pushing into a sprint so that Cat's bumped First and Third Trinity opposite Stourbridge Common and went Head of the River. When the crew pulled to the bank to celebrate, Coats refused to release his oar. Not even the big men in the middle of the boat could pry his hands loose, and when the crew lifted Coats from the shell and stretched him out on the grass for the celebration, bow and number two unlocked the oar and carrying the blade gingerly and reverently put it on a flat bare spot so Coats could row comfortably.

Cat's had never gone Head of the River before; cigars were passed around and champagne flowed. While the crew danced about, boozing and thumping one another on the back, Coats lay on his side in the grass, thrusting and grunting and puffing on a cigar the cox had stuffed in his mouth. The crew knew they could not have succeeded without Coats, and they wanted his corpse to enjoy the celebration. When the ambulance came to cart him off, they gathered around him, taking care of course not to be hit by his oar, and sang "For He's a Jolly Good Fellow." Not until rigor mortis set in eight hours later did Coats stop rowing, and the undertaker, a Cat's and rowing man himself, said that just before Coats let go of his oar forever he raised the rhythm to a magnificent fifty-four strokes per minute. In retrospect, I suppose the person who tells such a tale does not understand the high nature of sport. What I do know is that in school, playing is play and is vastly more important than winning.

Ambition

If poor spellers or stumbling mathematicians show no interest in the other languages to which you introduce them—that of the shoreline, waves green with life, or that of trees, birdsong slapping through leaves in blue shards—don't be discouraged. Children often succeed, not always in ways that schools and teachers recognize but in ways they can be proud of. Moreover the appointments of some school districts are so harsh that successes are difficult. Sloganeering does not eradicate drugs. Words help but not so much as money and police. Studies of educational achievement inevitably distort. A school in a poor district may be accomplishing more educationally and socially than a school in a wealthy district. Yet because of children's lives at home and countless other factors, students from the wealthy district will likely score higher on standardized tests than those from the poor district, creating the superficial impression that the school in the affluent area is far better than that in the poor area.

Tight shoes pave dirt roads and raise blisters. When your efforts to broaden students seem failures, the best you can do is relax for a moment. Kick your shoes off and wiggle your toes in the dirt. Something in class will soon delight and invigorate you.

This fall I stepped on a walnut while jogging and transformed my ankle into a blood orange. For six weeks I did not jog, and if students had not entertained me I might have slipped into gloom. One day when the world seemed especially dark and confining, I read a student's paper. Optimism shone from the page, making me smile and look forward to my next class. The girl wrote an essay about cooking. "If you put me in a kitchen," she wrote, "with a few bowls, measuring cups, teaspoons, some flour, sugar, eggs, margarine, oats, baking soda, baking powder, chocolate chips, and a recipe, in a few hours out will come a happy girl and some delicious cookies." "Oh, yes," I thought. "I ought to introduce her to Edward." The next paper I read made me laugh. In the essay Tyler described an inspirational speaker, writing, "She directs from her breast a voice of spirited zeal that I marvel at." "As well you should marvel," I wrote in the margin beside the sentence. "Rarely do breasts speak. Most lack vocal cords." "Don't you think that a bit strong?" Vicki said. "Certainly not," I said. "I am just trying to be anatomically correct."

Even if nothing you say or do invigorates students and you think your class a failure, you might be wrong. Whenever I attempt to analyze the effects of my teaching, a story about a Harvard entomologist comes to mind. The man studied fleas for two decades, finally teaching them to jump when he said "hop." After the fleas learned to obey the command, the scientist sliced off the insects' legs. Immediately the fleas stopped jumping, no matter how loudly the scientist yelled. After analyzing data for twenty-six months, the scientist concluded that the reason the fleas had ceased hopping was that they heard with their legs. "Once the specimens' tibias were removed," the scientist wrote in the *New England Journal of Medicine*, "they were deaf. Although I spent a year trying to teach *Pulex irritans* sign language, I was not successful."

Know your classes well, but don't live vicariously through students. If you do you will be disappointed. Some of you will be so disappointed that you will retreat or, on the positive side, march into administration. Teachers become administrators for many reasons. Some are good at it. Some resemble missionaries. Duty motivates them, and they hope administration will enable them to affect reforms that will better not only a class but a neighborhood, even a city. Some people just want more money. Others are seduced by the illusion of power. Still others want to change their lives and think administration will buck them up.

Additionally metaphors describing life in America seduce many people. Almost from the moment they pop out of the womb Americans hear patter about getting ahead, climbing ladders, and being somebody. To decide not to pursue what appears to be advancement seems almost un-American, at the least stamping one as indulgent or a ne'er-do-well. Think long before you shift your life into administration, however. Certainly the prospect of teaching the same course until the undertaker knocks on your door can appear grim. Assuredly the prospect will be grim if you can't imagine ever changing the course or teaching new courses. Classroom life, however, is marvelously rich and rewarding, not something to be pushed aside thoughtlessly.

As I said earlier, I once pondered college presidencies. I went for interviews, but I was too selfish to become a college president. I enjoyed the pleasures of family and class too much to give them up. Of course the trips I took were fun, and I returned to the classroom invigorated. At one school a trustee took me to a picnic. Immediately before the picnic I'd met administrators, and I arrived at the picnic in a three-piece suit. The trustee parked his car in a pasture and I changed clothes beside his car. Under the trousers to my suit I wore boxer shorts decorated with small green cats. On seeing the shorts the man said, "I've seen it all now." "You've seen most of it," I responded, "but certainly not all."

Oddity

If you eschew administration and remain in the classroom, you must develop hobbies that thrust you into the company of adults. If you don't, you may lose quickness and become dull, first to colleagues then perhaps to students themselves. I started writing essays for myself. As a college teacher I had free time, and I did not want to think myself a layabout. I also began to write because forcing thought into paragraphs disciplined my mind and made days bloom with observation. The classroom distorts, and after a decade of startling the young, teachers can lose perspective on themselves and on life itself. Students' thoughts can interest and startle, but they should not constitute the only course of an adult's intellectual diet.

Undergraduates think shadows luminous. Write two articles and undergraduates will think you Milton, one poem and you become Wordsworth. A year after returning to the United States from teaching in Jordan I wrote Joseph, one of my former students. I mentioned I was writing a book. "How happy I was," he answered, "and still to receive a letter from you. I read it thrice, or more, enjoying your words as if you were present and talking with me. Through your words and lines, I draw a very beautiful picture of your face. I am happy to know," he continued, "that you are writing some books. I wish for you a very bright future in writings. I hope that you will be as prominent as Shakespeare one day." Essay writing forced me into a rugged, judgmental, adult landscape. If I had not written books, when the *Dead Poets Society* appeared I would have felt like a fraud. Although I had nothing to do with the movie, my books sat on a desk and were real. Although the books did not give me much stature, they provided the appearance of substance. I was not just another person riding out of anonymity on the back of someone else's achievement, a lottery winner receiving something for nothing.

Willful

Vicki calls me the apostle of the mundane. Being such an apostle is not bad for a husband or a teacher, particularly if the mundane is associated with the responsible. I am always responsible, so much so my daughter calls me Rasputin and accuses me of being too conservative and controlling. Still, beyond the family, at least, I am willful. To keep my mind pulsating outside class and then indirectly in class, I not only prepare lessons but also toy with words. I write something every week. Rarely do I enter a classroom without thoughts tumbling about. The stir enlivens class and attracts students. In between writing I play word games. Because I am not an administrator and don't feel compelled to conform to someone's idea of proper, usually dead, behavior, I am free to follow whim. Every January friends of the local library sponsor a book sale. Residents both donate and buy books, and proceeds from the sale support future library purchases. I always donate a box of books to the sale. Good books delight and intrigue. Unfortunately some of my books are dully cerebral. To tart them up, I inscribe the books. "To Achilles," I wrote on the title page of one book. "In memory of the night we spent together at the bathhouse. You have my word Clara will never know. Love, Patroclus, your own little coochie-coo." "Blithe," I wrote in another book. "Can you believe that thirty years have passed since the seventies? You and I both have families. But sometimes I wonder what happened to our love child. She is now almost grown. How foolish and young, yet how loving we were. Your Spotty."

Occasionally I compose fictional articles then cite them as sources in an essay. In *Antiquities Now and Then,* for example, I recently read an article claiming mistranslation distorted the story of Zeus and Leda. Instead of mating with Leda in the guise of a swan, Zeus actually visited Leda disguised as a chicken. Although the coupling produced a blue-ribbon egg, double-yoked with

Helen and Pollux, the couple's love was an earthier barnyard affair than devotees to matters Hellenic are accustomed to believing. "Thinking of Zeus as a chicken," the author wrote in *A N & T,* "demystifies Paris's infatuation with Helen and should spur critics to reexamine the Trojan conflict, the celebration of which has long been a keystone of classical education."

Several times a year I compose crank letters. Although I think my suggestions on most matters to be sound, perhaps you should avoid crank letters. If you write one, send it only to someone you have known well for twenty years. If you are a male, do not write a female. If you are a female, don't send your letter to a male. Males are slow to rise to wit, and you will be misunderstood. Do not use untoward language, and do not say anything that might frighten. Include clues that reveal the letter as bogus. Your reader won't notice them but include them anyway. Nine years ago my son Edward played on the town's twelve-and-under soccer team. On Memorial Day the team participated in a tournament near Danbury. The referee of the first game was poor. Rarely did he shift his position from midfield, and only occasionally did he look at the line judges. Near the end of the second half, a friend and father of one of Edward's teammates stepped onto the edge of the field and called the referee a turkey. Immediately the referee forfeited the game to the other side. An artist, the father was a mild man, and the referee's action provoked laughter more than exasperation. Three nights later I sent a letter to the father.

Francis created the letterhead for me on the computer: a black-and-white soccer ball three and a half inches in diameter.

Circling the ball in bold black letters were the words "Connecticut Soccer Association." Supposedly the writer of the letter was Annette D. Barcombaker, Worthy Grand Matron of the "CSAss" and a resident of 476 Post Hole Road in Darien. "Dear Mr. Todd," the letter began. "This morning I received a letter from Mr. R. F. (Fred) Jaggerson, director of the Newtown Kick-Off Tournament. Fred informs me that during the past weekend you used fowl language on the athletic field, calling one of the referees a turkey. Actually I understand that the phrase used was more personal and you said 'you turkey' to Mr. Igot Highballs, one of our most respected officials. The use of such language is reprehensible. If you had called Mr. Highballs a coxcomb, we at the association would be more understanding. But to give a man of his distinguished appearance the bird is shocking. By the way did you hear about the sick man whose doctor advised him to eat a piece of pullet? The man refused, saying it might 'lay' on his stomach. Ha, ha! We at the association are a lively flock. There are no flies on our giblets.

"I can only assume," the letter continued, "that hormones triggered your behavior. Are you middle-aged, Mr. Todd? Many soccer fathers your age experience problems with testosterone. I recall that on one occasion a former All-American football player and the father of a lovely blond child aged twelve started growing breasts after he passed thirty-eight. From this distance I do not presume to analyze the effects of hormones upon you, but I do advise you to seek professional help. Fred tells me that not only did you call the official a turkey but you stepped upon the field to do so. Only once before has one of our fathers violated a field to address an official. This happened in 1986, as I recollect, during the first half of a game between the Greenwich Bandits and the Milford Darlings. Like you the man was an artist. He encroached upon the field not to criticize but because he was overcome with passion. The official that day was Mr. Billy Capon, a man with the most divine buns and who played the organ at St. George's Episcopal Church in Woodbridge.

"The father couldn't control his lust, and he embraced Mr. Billy near the thirty-yard marker, disrupting a breakaway. All ended happily, however. He and Mr. Billy eloped the next day. They now own an antique shop in Westport. As I recall the man behaved a great deal like you, calling Mr. Billy 'my itsy-bitsy turkey gobbler.' Mr. Todd, examine your motives for stepping on the field. Did desire master reason? I leave the probing of your parts to you alone. I must now stop to prepare Cornish hen for my beloved spouse. But I want to stress that all of us in the Connecticut Soccer Ass. are praying for you. We think of you as a member of our extended family."

How long did it take my recipient to realize that someone was tickling his crop? Six readings and two full days.

Letter Six: Truth

DEAR TEACHER,

Truth has long interested me, both in the classroom and without. Truth and falsehood wind through creativity, teaching, and daily life like fat through beef, seasoning and enriching. From one perspective the more cultured and more sensitive people are the more they lie. Concerned, maybe overly so, about decency and civility, the liar values the particular more than the abstract. Weaving fancy across the gulf separating what is from what could be or perhaps ought to be, teachers distort, if they do not lie, nurturing hope and dream. Teachers know that today's failing student might become tomorrow's passing student, and in order not to smother dormant ability they encourage and soften harsh truth. For the teacher and the liar, life is not a pilgrimage but a meandering, freeing people from the straight and narrow. Teachers urge classes to stray into strange, for students at least, fields of thought in hopes that they will learn and develop. Oddly, and perhaps sadly, only after they learn to lie or say so little that they practically live a lie can children have lives of their own. Towering over the child, the ogreish parent says, "I can forgive anything but a lie"—a statement that is itself a lie.

Not just crank letters but lies sail through my books, classes, and life like Frisbees. Pony Boguski was the most notorious miser in Carthage. Some years ago Pony had his tonsils removed at Baptist Hospital in Nashville. After the operation Pony telegraphed his wife, Little Robin. Western Union did not charge customers for their names. "I want to wire Carthage," Pony said to the operator. "What's your name?" the operator asked. "Well," Pony said, "I know I look a little pale, but I'm a Cherokee Indian, and I've just had an operation. My Christian name is 'I-Will-Be-Home-Friday.' My middle name is 'On-the-Evening-Train,' and my last name is 'Hold-Dinner-and-Meet-Me-on-the-Platform-at-Eight-O'clock.'"

Many things contribute to good classes: preparation, discipline, mood, trust, understandings shared between students and teachers, and, yes, if not lies, exaggerations and distortions. Despite what sometimes seems a drumbeat extolling the virtue of truthfulness, adults know, as the maxim states, anyone who tells the truth ought to keep one foot in the stirrup. The mother who preaches the importance of truth at breakfast tapes her daughter's drawing to the refrigerator door after dinner. Although the picture resembles a squirrel that has dozed for a week in the middle of an interstate, the mother praises her baby, kissing her, and says, "This is so beautiful. Maybe someday you will be an artist."

Honesty threatens the fictions people erect to make social life possible, not to mention love. Belief, whether right or wrong, supports culture, and if people begin to wander far from accepted paths and tell hard truths, community shatters. What most of us do is what I often did on the school board: listen, mumble to myself, and say nothing. Occasionally I broke into truth, or at least a half-truth. Afterward I apologized. At one meeting we discussed reining in programs for the "gifted." Not only is almost every child gifted in some way, a way frequently not measured by schools, but every family in an academic community believes their children gifted. As a result pressure grew not to neglect any child and increase enrollment in programs for the gifted. In middle-class communities parents are aggressively ambitious, and programs for the gifted often swell out of identity and academic effectiveness. At a meeting when the board pondered restricting access to programs for the gifted, a well-meaning parent spoke and urged us to expand not limit the programs, arguing that talented children needed to be challenged. If not, they would be stifled, and they would become bored and lose interest in school. "Madame," I said when the woman finished speaking, "don't you realize that coping with boredom is the greatest challenge of life. Boredom does not stifle; it fosters creativity. If we were really committed to challenging students, we would stop entertaining them and start boring the hell out of them. If we did so, perhaps they would think on their own and wander beyond stifling conventional thought. Maybe we would then have schools full of Newtons and Shakespeares. At the least we would be preparing students for life beyond school, most of which is unendingly, reassuringly boring."

The impulse toward disorder runs deep in thinking people, especially so in teachers whose classes depend heavily upon order, an order that sometimes seems remarkably artificial. Graduation speakers forever declare and college faculty genuflect before the statement that "College prepares students for life." Although classes may help a person to become an accountant or English teacher, the school day itself is surreal, resembling the chaos on the front page of a newspaper, a column here describing the horrors of monsoon floods on the subcontinent, a picture of a girl shooting a basketball, a column dizzy with the assertions of a political spin doctor, an interview with a mother of an only son killed in a foreign war, gossip about a celebrity's marriage and his new affair—the sociology of poverty at eight in the morning; at nine an English class discussing Emerson and Nature in New England; next statistics, followed by lunch, coffee, gossip, then an entomology lab.

Dull men govern, and if you want to achieve success as measured by bureaucracies, school or otherwise, you cannot always be a contrarian. You must smother objection and statements to the effect that life is complex. Lives resemble houses. Into one room we stuff the doings of job; into the closet the past; in another room family activities. Cram your antisocial nature into an attic or work shed. Find, as I suggested earlier, interests that enable you to stretch and wander far from bureaucratic rigor mortis. Your classes will be livelier, and you will be better able to endure hours sealed in bureaucratic envelopes. Breaking out, however, is always difficult to resist. Strangely enough, even when we do shred the envelope and say the unthinkable, and maybe the obvious, we feel guilty, almost as if we have betrayed a trust.

Near the end of my term, the school board set seven goals for the school system, one of which was to increase children's "motivation to learn," boilerplate to convince us, and the one or two members of the public that noticed such things, that we were accomplishing and improving. Behind the boilerplate, of course, teachers had to stoke small visible fires. At a later meeting a principal provided a list of things done at his school to increase motivation. On the list was "Greeting Students When They Arrive at School." Of course the principal was trying to make children feel comfortable and not regret having left home. Still, I said, after reading the list, "What sort of greeting do you use? Do you say 'Good morning, you little son of a bitch?'" When the principal looked startled, I forged ahead. "When my children get off the bus in the afternoon, I say, 'Welcome home, you little bastards. How was the Hell Hole today.' And," I continued, "I'm giving my babies something important: the ability to deal with the unexpected. In contrast to all those other children greeted by a bland, simpering 'Good morning, Johnny' or 'Did you have a nice day, Sally?' my babies are learning to cope. Instead of being startled and knocked off stride by the unforeseeable, my children will hunker down and batter ahead, straight through to success."

Although such a remark may touch partial truths and provide the speaker with a selfish momentary satisfaction, it destroys rather than builds. If you can't avoid thinking such things, at least don't say them. Even if you do not mean to be cynical, such remarks enervate and smack of cynicism's slow, deadly poison. Besides, who would greet children as I said I did and, of course, did not? "Our principal was super," a student wrote, recollecting her elementary school. "Every day he stood at the door and greeted us when we came off the bus. He knew all our names, and when he said 'Good morning,' we knew the day was going to be good."

On most occasions teachers have to be cheerleaders and kick up their heels over optimistic distortion and flawed truth. If you are unable to live in a compromised world, you should not teach. Life is too various for stringency. In class I emphasize that students' papers must be their own. I mention honor and integrity. Yet cultures vary, and there are circumstances in which honor, as we in the West define it, is not a major virtue. In Jordan loyalty to community is more important. Not to let a friend look at, and copy, one's paper would undermine family and its rich web of responsibilities to others. The first time I assigned a paper in Jordan, four students handed in the same essay. I called Hashem into my office and asked him where he got the paper. "Allah gave it to me," he answered. "There must be a copying machine in heaven then," I said, leaning forward aggressively. "Three of your classmates turned in the same paper." Hashem paused, folded his hands together in his lap, and rolled his eyes toward the ceiling before replying. "Ah, sir," he said, "there are many true believers in the class. Allah is merciful and compassionate and would not forget them." Hashem and his friends passed, and the next time I assigned a paper I gave each student a different topic.

When Hashem left my office, I laughed. Culture aside, he was in part a familiar, even beloved, character, the trickster. The main characters of many folktales and children's books are trick-sters. The trickster is the hero of the disenfranchised and the weak. In fact the trickster may be the most universal hero in literature. The trickster's triumph is not simply that of the weak rabbit over the strong fox, the slave over the master, the little and neglected over the big and favored, but that of all people who in this world of multinational corporations and faceless, inhuman governments think themselves impotent. "Bred and bawn in a brier patch" is more than the taunt of a weak crea-ture in a folktale. It is the cry we all want to give when cun-ning enables us to "beat the odds."

This past summer Eliza worked in Vergas, Minnesota, teach-ing Russian in a camp run by Concordia University. I bought Eliza a round-trip airplane ticket from Hartford to Fargo, North Dakota. Both coming and going Eliza changed planes in Min-neapolis. At summer's end she spent two days in Minneapolis with the family of a friend she had met at camp. When Eliza went to the airport in Minneapolis, the airline representative refused to allow Eliza to board the plane. If a person bought a round-trip ticket to Fargo, the representative explained, she had to fly from Fargo and could not board at the next stop. "The rule was ab-surd," Eliza said. "What did you do?" I asked. "I remembered *Uncle Remus*," Eliza said. "I told the airline representative that I came to Minneapolis to visit my uncle. This morning he was supposed to drive me to Fargo. Unfortunately he left the house after breakfast to buy me a going-home present. While on the way to the store, he was in a car wreck. A man ran a stop sign and smashed into him. At this point," Eliza continued, "I pinched the tip of my nose just under the eyes with my thumb and index finger, looking as if I were damming tears." "Oh, my," the representative said, "how is your uncle?" "He has a broken arm and leg," Eliza said, "but he is going to be all right. Thank goodness he was driving a Volvo." "You poor dear," the representative said, "don't worry. I'll make sure you get on the airplane. Now you just sit down and rest until your flight is called." "Was what Eliza did right?" Vicki asked later. "Of course," I said. "The rule was unreasonable. I paid for Eliza's ticket. So she didn't use part of it. People don't finish meals in restaurants. People leave football games at halftime. Truth would not have brought Eliza home on schedule."

As the saying puts it, there are lies and damn lies, as there are truths and damn truths. I suspect that if pushed to discuss lies in public most people would draw the line at lying for money. I would, but then books and years in schools have taught me a lot, and I have lied for money and would do so again, provided the amount was not insignificant. In 1963 I spent the last week of December in Sofia, Bulgaria. I arrived in Sofia on Christmas day on the early morning train from Bucharest. I was a student and didn't have much money. I could not afford to pay ten dollars a day for a room in a tourist hotel. I walked the streets until I discovered the World Student Association, its office windows decorated with anti-American posters. "Just the group to find me a hotel," I thought and stepped into the building. After I told the director that I was a young Communist from the United States,

he found me a room for fifty cents a night. The room was modest in cost but immodest, or at least the activities that occurred
inside were immodest. The door lacked a lock. After I talked to
him in the hall, an Indian gentleman living next door conceived
a passion for me. Three times during the night he burst into my
room, naked and in a state of considerable excitement. Each time
I escorted him back to his room, though by the last occasion I
was slightly irritated as I was sleepy and high jinks of the sort he
proposed have never interested me.

Our appreciation and celebration of the trickster and our
own slippery behaviors complicate our attitude toward truth, and
so we temporize. Without hypocrisy or, to put a better word on
the matter, inconsistency, social life is impossible. The classroom,
however, often inflates dishonesty. Indeed no one could teach a
class of congenital liars. Of particular concern to higher education is plagiarism, foisting off another's words as one's own. Plagiarism can be as destructive to a university career as adultery can
be to a marriage. Students usually receive F's in the courses in
which they plagiarize and are often suspended from the university. No teacher I know tolerates plagiarism. Yet, and herein lies
the problem, society's attitude toward this sort of cheating is
mixed. Like many cultures we punish the youngest and the weak-
est for what is standard operating procedure among adults. Books
and speeches are ghostwritten. Many presidents of the United
States did not write their State of the Union addresses. College
CEOs have speechwriters. Is the only reason teenagers are pe-
nalized for doing what corporate and political America routinely

does is that teenagers are comparatively weak? John Kennedy won the Pulitzer Prize for *Profiles in Courage,* a book he did not write. A team of two dozen people wrote Ronald Reagan's memoir *An American Life.* "I hear it is a terrific book," Reagan is supposed to have said after its publication. "One of these days I am going to read it myself." So that I won't be thought a plagiarist, let me state now that I pulled this information from John Maxwell Hamilton's *Casanova Was a Book Lover.*

In the face of blatant cheating by the most successful adults in the nation, how should teachers behave? In years past, higher education seemed slightly otherworldly. Universities were not so corporate. Because universities generally did not seem arms of commercial life, people sometimes paid attention to what university and educational leaders said. At times such leaders rose above low frays and seemed voices of morality, decency, and reason. Rarely does anyone listen to a university president today. Speeches are tissues of platitude, structured not to say and thus not to irritate vested financial or political interests. As naive as this may sound, I think teachers should try to recapture the moral high ground, this despite knowing that little in life is clean-cut. In class we shouldn't accept dishonesty and plagiarism. We should not accept dishonesty in society itself, but that is another matter. By the same token, truth, as I have tried to point out, is not a simple concept or behavior. Pondering it is confusing. Because we teach children, we should be firm but kind, especially in elementary and high school. Although students will listen to you, the behavior of successful, highly visible adults will undermine what you say, and you must be patient. Explain and explain again. Make students rewrite. Even though you may become angry, resist resentment and the accompanying inclination toward severity.

Students, particularly young students, are not always responsible for their behavior. No matter their ostensible high purposes, adults should not impose impossible standards on children. For that reason I oppose honor codes in secondary schools. Supervising tests closely is laborious and demeaning, but it is a clean way of preventing dishonesty. Instead of forcing students to shoulder the burden of honesty and in the process perhaps disappointing a parent, teachers should lighten their students' loads and monitor tests and, if possible, papers. I thought the honor code at MBA repulsive, if not immoral. In 1955 when I entered high school, the honor system had been established at the school for a decade. Copied from the University of Virginia, the code purported to promote honor among students by punishing stealing, lying, and cheating. In practice the system took hard shape. A flawed, cruel presence enabling people to do the easy thing and measure fault by rule rather than mind or heart, the honor system should never have been applied to adolescents. After having been caught cheating on more than one occasion, a student was usually forced to apologize to the entire school at assembly. Ostensibly corrective and edifying, the scene was destructive. Not only did it affect the boy apologizing, stripping him of dignity and privacy, often reducing him to tears, but it also marked those of us forced to listen in ways that supporters of the honor code probably had not imagined. The scenes made me aware of the inhumanity of rule and principle and soured the word *honor.*

Instead of humiliating a child, you should talk to parents, generally the force pressuring a child to cheat. Above all you must stay alert, something made more onerous by the Internet. Because papers are available by the bushel on the Internet, you must tailor assignments accordingly. In my poetry class we read old favorites, but I assign papers only on good but obscure poets, poets on whose work no papers are available. For extra credit in my short story class students can write a story. I monitor their progress carefully. I require that two rough drafts of the story be turned in with the final copy. I ask students to submit first drafts to me. In the attempt to slip Internet papers past me, some students ignore my instructions and hand in all copies of their papers at once. Students are naive and careless, particularly those who cheat. So far, I think, no one has succeeded in getting credit for the fraudulent. Last semester a boy handed in a fairy tale placed in Turkey. In the first two paragraphs the heroine's name was Rosara. For the next five pages she was Fatima. In the last paragraph she once again became Rosara. The first draft of a girl's paper was very good and did not contain a single spelling or grammar error, something the girl rectified in the second draft, in which she introduced a wheelbarrow of illiteracies. By the final copy the paper was an incomprehensible farrago of errors. "Ah, the dangers of purloining," Josh said. "Perhaps schools should offer courses in 'Revising the Internet Paper.'"

Grammar and Words

"Mr. Pickering," the reporter from the *Hartford Courant* began, "the new edition of the *Oxford American Desk Dictionary* accepts the split infinitive. What's your reaction?" When the reporter telephoned I was pushing my foot down the left leg of a worn pair of trousers. Earlier I had cleaned the air filter on my lawn mower, readying myself to mulch leaves, not verbs. As I pulled up the trousers I almost said, "I don't give a fart about infinitives." Then for a moment I pondered a serious answer, saying the vitality of English depended upon democracy. Rules changed with seasons. Like mushrooms in fall, words suddenly appeared, some spilling spores through the language, others vanishing overnight, being cropped by the voles and squirrels of usage. English sprawled vulgar and alive, unlike French, which academicians labored to freeze into propriety, deadening it cryogenically at the top in hopes of insulating it against change. Because people skim newspapers, however, I jettisoned the thoughtful for the brisk and said, "I do not dine with those who split infinitives." And that remark, I thought, slapped a declarative end on the subject.

I was wrong. Although grammar has evolved as arbitrarily and as strangely as the duck-billed platypus, violations of what people think is proper grammar causes greater turmoil for teachers than does controversy over truth and plagiarism. Grammar is always changing, something that disturbs parents, school boards, and conservative social critics. Into changes in grammar critics read dire social consequences, crying, "As the sentence goes, so goes the nation." After my comment appeared in the *Courant,* I received baskets of letters and transformers of e-mail. The Associated Press reprinted my quip. *Newsday* made it "Quote of the Day," and a score of radio programs interviewed me. Rarely do remarks on radio constitute a sound bite, so I cooked up several crisp statements. I began interviews with "To be or to not be, that is the question." "Republicans," I said, "had mulled making me an independent linguistic prosecutor." On some shows I declared my patriotism, asking why an *Oxford* dictionary. "Why not a Nashville, a Wichita, or a Peckerwood Point dictionary, containing apple-pie American speech?" Unfortunately my literary petits fours rarely sweetened interviewers. Nobody recognized the paraphrase of *Hamlet.* "Is that a quote?" a man asked. "Yes," I answered. "What's it from?" he continued. "It sounds good, but what does it mean?" "I've heard of Nashville and Wichita," a woman said, "but not Peckerwood Point. In what state is it located?" "Wow," a woman said, "I didn't think people in Congress cared enough about education to appoint a linguistic prosecutor."

You will find that discussions of language short-circuit common sense. Many e-mails I received bristled, my correspondents not seeing humor but elitism. In general people take matters of language and grammar more seriously perhaps than they do going to war. Several e-mails were insulting. "Dear Anonymous," I wrote one particularly nasty correspondent, "you didn't sign your name. What a pitiful chickenshit you are." Eliza saw my reply. "Don't send that, Daddy," she said. "The person is so angry he

is liable to appear in Storrs and lay addled eggs on the front stoop."
Other correspondents praised me. "I am glad someone maintains
high standards in the classroom," a man wrote. "Standards are so
low today that a one-legged grasshopper could bound over them."
Under the heading DISAPPOINTMENT, a woman wrote, "It
has come to my attention a horrible quote attributed to you in a
recent AP news update regarding the latest edition of OED. The
article quoted you as saying that you do not dine with those who
split infinitives. I would hope this is not true and if it is, it was in
jest. How crude it would be to say such a thing in real life; removing oneself from opportunities to dine with those would
benefit perhaps from your life experiences. Have you ever taken
it upon yourself to dine with children or young adults who would
benefit from educated mentors and perhaps imbed a spark in a
young mind to succeed in life? Would that be possible if you were
only to dine with those who avoid splitting infinitives? How
unaccomplished your life must be to be so haughty and removed."
In contrast to letters from people suffering from fused intelligences,
several messages flickered good-naturedly. "I saw your remark
about the infinitive in *Newsweek*," a woman wrote from California. "In June I heard you give a commencement address. In the
speech you mentioned a son but not a wife. Might you be single?"

I am too old for illicit grammatical couplings. Despite believing most grammar arbitrary and even silly, I am a grammatical conservative. To some extent grammar rules like social
manners are devices that exclude, rather than include, and which
perpetrate those in power and in the know, providing them with

a way to discriminate. How a person holds a knife and fork reveals nothing about his soul and is, in any great perspective, meaningless. Yet we do not live in the great perspective. We live in a little now, and so I take knives and forks to class and show students how to handle them properly. For a decade I ruined my children's meals, lecturing on table manners and speech, among other things, forbidding them to say "like" like the mythic California girl and forcing them to use *lie* and *lay* "correctly," although I realize that so few people pay attention to standard usage that the standard is no longer standard. As a teacher, you should be aware of and appreciate the flux of language and usage. But in class you should err on the side of conservatism. What is learned can usually be pitched aside easily. Sometimes what is left unlearned becomes a barrier blocking advancement. Good teachers enable students to function comfortably in various worlds. Not being at ease with standard usage may inhibit. An old standby puts the matter obliquely. "It is better to have a little too much than a little too little because it is harder to raise a little too little up to a little too much than it is to pull a little too much down to a little too little."

In order to teach we distort. "Faith, hope, and clarity," a teacher of mine used to say, describing writing, "but the greatest of these is clarity." I advise students to write simple short sentences. I stress the importance of clarity. The truth is that life is complex, composed not of simple sentences or clarity, but confusion—run-on paragraphs, dangling moods and modifiers, and conjunctions that connect nothing. We impose order and create institutions that impose order because living in the absence of meaning and structure is too difficult. Then ironically the practices that we shape in order to be able to function begin to shape us. Twenty-five years of writing short declarative sentences have affected my personality. Putting periods where they should not be, thus shutting down thought before complexity intrudes, has made me cranky and opinionated. Who knows what effect, if any, the classroom's celebration of clarity and the short sentence has had upon national life? Perhaps it has made us simpleminded. Perhaps it has made us impatient and so constitutionally allergic to complexity that we act too swiftly with what other countries see as arrogant certainty.

To say that composing sentences leads to composing lives is probably over the top. Nevertheless, if you teach, you should ponder words and their effects. In *Through the Looking-Glass,* Alice wandered into a wood "where things have no names." A fawn met her, but because the fawn did not know Alice was a human, the fawn was not afraid. Alice clasped her arms "lovingly around the soft neck of the Fawn," and the two ambled along happily together until they reached the border of the wood. Once they stepped outside the wood, the fawn looked at her companion and realized Alice was a human. "A sudden look of alarm," Lewis Carroll wrote, "came into its beautiful brown eyes, and in another moment it had darted away at full speed." Suppose we lived in a world not of no names but a world in which words that pin us to poster boards like insects and make us enemies of one another disappeared, all those words that divide: denominational words of all sorts, religious and ethnic. Suppose we were just people, not Palestinian and Israeli, Catholic and Protestant, Tutsi and Hutu, Serbian and Albanian, black and white. Those of you who teach reading and writing must look beyond letters to effects. Does this statement imply that I advocate censorship? No, certainly not a censorship imposed by a bureaucracy that will invariably be so simpleminded that it is wrong, probably even evil. But you should exercise a thoughtful control, one of your making.

In *The Invisible Pyramid,* Loren Eiseley said that language is "by its very necessity limiting" and has created for man "an invisible prison. . . . Language implies boundaries. A word spoken creates a dog, a rabbit, a man. It fixes their nature before our eyes; henceforth their shapes are, in a sense, our creation. They are no longer part of the unnamed shifting architecture of the universe. They have been transfixed as if by sorcery, frozen into a concept, a word. Powerful though the spell of human language has proven itself to be, it has laid boundaries upon the cosmos." Of course if you become so self-conscious that you believe every word you utter swings through class like a scythe, you will have to conduct lessons silently, with the result that your teaching career will be short-lived. What makes you thoughtful will affect you, but you cannot let it reduce enthusiasm and spontaneity to frass. As forgetfulness enabled Ratty and Mole to live normally after meeting Pan, so the multiple duties of teaching will keep you so busy that enervating self-doubt won't have much opportunity to bore through your day.

The irony is that words generally don't affect people the way you imagine they will. Once when I was bored and wanted to create a little stir and thus spice up a day or two, I wrote a piece in which I suggested creating departments of Ladies' Studies, saying that I found Women's Studies too fundamental for good taste, too bony and pelvic. I suggested courses in the marital arts, such as putting out the husband's slippers and baking fudge cake. I said I was tired of ignorance and wanted to be surrounded by females to the manor and manner educated, people who could recognize Coalport, Meissen, and Spode. I mentioned rugs, silver, and tapestries. In literature courses aspiring ladies would read such classics as *How to Succeed in Business Without Really Trying*. "This article will prove I am alive," I told Vicki. "When it appears, I'll receive a ton of mail." I was wrong. Dismal unending silence greeted the article. On the other hand, a character in another essay of mine while describing the toils of daily life mentioned *Anna Karenina* in passing, saying that once a person reached forty, living so sapped energy that he didn't have the strength to be concerned about Anna's motives and sufferings. "All that strumpet needed was a good spanking," he said. "I've got to sow grass seed today, and the yard is covered with sticks. When you spend your time picking up sticks and worrying about scraping the bottom of the car every time you back out of the garage, Karenina's doings don't mean much." Shortly after the essay appeared, I received a furious letter. "What sort of person are you—advocating beating women?" my correspondent wrote. "You are a disgrace."

As a teacher you cannot escape being misunderstood. Even if you are quoted accurately, people will misunderstand. Confusion is built into language. In *Alice's Adventures in Wonderland,* the King becomes angry at the Mad Hatter because he thinks the Hatter said *t* when in fact the Hatter said *tea.* "That reminds me of the story about a man with two monkeys, named Wilbur and Alice," my father once said in response to a misinterpretation. "One winter," Father recounted, "Wilbur and Alice caught influenza and died. Their owner, an aging bachelor, was so attached to them he couldn't bear to live without them, so he took them to a taxidermist to have them stuffed. 'Would you like them mounted?' the taxidermist asked. 'That's mighty kind of you to think of that,' the old man replied. 'Wilbur and Alice were close, but I believe I'd just prefer them holding hands.'"

Although words are tools and although their use can have important implications, words are also playthings. As math teachers should make classes so familiar with numbers that students enjoy playing with them, so English teachers should convey the joy of words. In my books after lengthy descriptions of mushrooms or spiders or after pondering matters that frighten or worry me, I drain sense from my pen and refill it with play. Every year in my fictional world Tennessee Democrats in the state legislature hold a convention in the Grand Hotel in Red Boiling Springs. Old friends Squirrel Tomkins and Coker Knox have long sat in the legislature. One year Squirrel was in line for lieutenant governor. Unfortunately, Squirrel drank away the nomination. Afterward he went on the wagon. Early the first morning at

the convention the following year Squirrel met Coker in the bathroom on the second floor of the Grand. A year can bring great
changes. During the winter Coker had taken a course in poetry
at the YMCA night school in Nashville. While Squirrel was now
sober, Coker soared aloft on the divine afflatus.

"Ah, Nature is a real artist," Coker said, shooing the flies
away with his right hand before waxing poetic. "The sunrise is
obstetric," he hymned. "The lambent flame of life skipping
odalisque over the bosom of the world, the wild wood grape
gleaming through the grove dappled with waves of dew, the azure
breeze soothing the slumber of the weary marsupial, the velveted
reveler murmuring above the festal dainties of the woodland
board, our feathered friends warbling their sonorous notes ver-
milion and crepuscular, the bosky tortoise munching the ruddy
nightshade, the brown cow letting down her milk, the downy
chicks hopping from under the incubator to seek a better worm.
Squirrel, my dear, dear Squirrel," Coker said, "have you never
stood bareheaded before the rising sun and had such thoughts?"
"Not," Squirrel said, turning back from the wall and fastening a
last button or two, "since I stopped drinking."

Letter Seven: Plans

DEAR TEACHER,

Forty years ago in graduate school—before rakes and lawn mowers, strollers and car seats, gardening and college tuition—my friends and I spent much energy contemplating amorous adventures. We laid wonderfully ornate plans and had marvelous conversational times. The only thing that eluded us was success, in some ways the thing that mattered least. One morning a physicist joined me at breakfast. He was excited and waved a piece of paper over his eggs and bacon. "I have it now," he said. "The Eighteen Steps to Seduction, drawn up according to scientific method and guaranteed not to fail." "What are the steps?" I asked. "Never mind," he said. "Tonight I am putting it to the test." The next morning at breakfast he looked a little glum. "How did the plan work?" I asked. "Oh that," he said. "I tripped on Step Two. Still," he said, brightening up a bit, "the plan itself is pretty good. A little tinkering will set it right." My friend never got the chance to return to the lab and tinker. A history student appeared at Princeton. She took one look at my friend, and without a single beaker, Bunsen burner, or plan, swept him off into marriage.

For teachers and students structure is important. If you do not plan days and subjects and set goals, you will drift and lose your class. Order lessons so that children believe they are accomplishing. Sow small achievements across weeks. People, even small people, think conventionally about their lives. They forever measure and see themselves climbing metaphoric ladders, bounding along fast lanes, forging ahead, or in medicinal terms getting better. Corporations and universities understand how people think, and to keep employees satisfied they create titles that convey the illusion of movement—in a university: lecturer, assistant professor, associate professor, professor, and distinguished professor. For administrators whose lives are not enriched by student admiration, titles are more important and, as a result, more numerous: assistant to the assistant provost, assistant provost, assistant to the associate provost, associate provost, assistant vice chancellor, associate vice chancellor, vice chancellor, assistant chancellor, associate chancellor, and chancellor. When sundry stripes of deans are tossed onto the page, one needs a guidebook to find his way through administration. To the neophyte the number of titles appears ludicrous. The initiated know, however, that titles are often more substantive than substance. For teachers the tendency of people to work for small recognition means they must plan. Build little rewards and acknowledgments into study plans.

When I was a boy I did not like to miss Sunday school, not because I enjoyed religious matters, not even drawing pictures of camels or having birthday parties for the baby Jesus, but because teachers kept charts of students' names in their rooms. When a child attended Sunday school, the teacher put a silver star beside his name. After ten Sundays a child received a gold star. We liked collecting stars, and competition grew as each child wanted his line of stars to be the longest in the class. By presenting awards for perfect attendance, schools appeal to the same compulsion in older children. From hindsight perfect attendance now seems almost emblematic of imperfection. If children are in the middle of good books or feel worn down, maybe they should stay home. I should add that I did not reach this conclusion on my own. My children forced me to it. Starting in the tenth grade, two of them began taking "mental health days," for Edward once every three weeks and for Eliza once every fortnight. Not having taught school, Vicki does not lie easily, and whenever a child stayed home I called the school with an excuse: sore throat, asthma again, low-grade fever, putrid sniffles, and menstrual cramps, among a general practitioner's office of ailments.

Plans are only guides. I plan essays carefully, usually spending three times more hours outlining than writing. On my outlines I jot down transitions, paradoxically often words and expressions that convey spontaneity—"unexpectedly," "suddenly," and "in the mail arrived." Do not follow plans slavishly. Direct your class and keep it close to schedule, but also let natural occurrence guide you. Indeed life, even life in the artificial environment of school, cannot be forced into a set pattern. Patterns are often supportive and reassuring, but if you are not comfortable outside of patterns and structure you will have trouble in class. Plans go wildly astray, frequently gloriously so. As the plotted nurtures creativity and fosters development, so it can inhibit. Creativity and growth also thrive amid the unstructured. Certainly we enjoy stories about people who triumph over hardship just because they are weedy, all the bad boys and girls of children's books who because they behave badly in school or the ordered world are good: Billy Whiskers the goat, William Green Hill, and Peck's Bad Boy hanging a sign in front of the grocery reading, CASH PAID FOR FAT DOGS.

Despite meticulous plotting no plan is adequate to education or to life. Two years ago a former student wrote me from the Rif Mountains in Morocco. After graduation Tom joined the Peace Corps. "I'm working on a reforestation effort," Tom recounted. "I give farmers olive trees to plant. They keep the money from their crops, and erosion in the area is slowed—at least that's how it is supposed to work. More often than not, farmers let their goats eat the olive trees, and they use the fertilizer I give them on marijuana plants. A Peace Corps Mission is often an exercise in futility."

Teaching also can be an exercise in futility. Days go terribly. Some students don't want to learn, and others appear incapable of learning. This January I met another former student on campus. When I'd taught her last spring she was pudgy. Now she was skinny. "You have lost a lot of weight," I said. I had seen her in the university swimming pool, so I continued, saying, "You must have swum a lot." "No," she said. "I did my student teaching this past fall. Anxiety, not exercise, made me lose weight." Anxiety and disappointment are also consorts of teaching. As a result many beginning teachers don't last long in the classroom. Teaching is hard. In some schools teaching is almost impossible. Teachers who endure must be sensitive, but they cannot be hypersensitive. They have to be able to shrug and push ahead through days. That is another reason why outside interests are important for teachers. They divert the mind from class and resemble recess. Playing lessens anxiety and invigorates.

"I still remember the tears running down her cheeks," Michael wrote in an essay. "Her name was Ms. Sullivan, and she broke down after only four hours in my seventh-grade class. She was young and pretty, but she was a rookie substitute. Even though she smiled when she took attendance, worry furrowed her brow, and we knew she had no idea what she was in for. She had entered the Snake Pit. As soon as we saw her, we realized she did not have the experience to handle our class." Normally, Michael wrote, the class was well behaved. The regular teacher, Mrs. Tull, was an older woman who did not tolerate disruption. While the substitute wore a soft pastel sweater and baggy trousers, Mrs. Tull wore form-fitting suits. While the substitute's nails were bitten almost to the quick, Mrs. Tull had razor-sharp red nails. "She waved her nails like bayonets," Michael continued, "and we behaved." Disobedience brought swift punishment. "A finger jabbed, and off we marched to the principal's office for a telephone call home. Because things were simple, we learned a lot, or at least I think we did. Mrs. Tull was the general. She gave the orders. We were the privates, and we obeyed." I asked my student if her experiences in the classroom had given her second thoughts about a teaching career. "No," she said, stiffening her back and looking straight through me like a graduate of officer's training school. "I learned a lot, and I can't wait to teach again."

Sloganeering makes it difficult for Americans to accept failure. We are surrounded by a drumbeat of slogans preaching that work can solve the unsolvable and make the impossible possible. Slogans often decorate locker rooms, such things as, "It's not the size of the dog in the fight that counts; it's the size of the fight in the dog" and "When the going gets tough, the tough get going." The rub is that outside of the imagination little dogs generally don't whip big dogs. If I had to wager on a fight between a dachshund and a mastiff, I'd put my money on the mastiff, even if he was the canine cousin of Ferdinand the Bull. When the going gets tough, the smart, I sometimes say, go elsewhere. "Unless your ancestors were slaves and were compelled to come to this country," I say, "you are the descendants of quitters, people whose existence in other places was so tough that they came here seeking better and easier lives. Instead of digging their cleats in and probably digging their graves, they quit and left."

Good teachers learn to accept failure. They don't have a choice. They will not better the lives of every student. "You can't," as the maxim puts it, "educate the twist out of the grapevine." Pressures upon teachers to educate are greater today, however, than they were when I was in school. "Our mothers," my friend Jeffrey wrote me recently, recalling our childhoods in Tennessee, "were wonderful blessings. They guided us with light hands and never asked us to grow up before we wanted to."

Changes in society have altered the ways in which people are identified. Because our society has grown more mobile, family and community do not identify us as they once did. Instead of being part of family and place, people have become their achievements and material goods. A wallet, car, house, or title measure a person and determine status. In some circles the schools people attend furnish identity, and people spend lives as fans. Arrested lives, I think, but that is another matter. People paste the names of their children's schools on automobile windows and insinuate the names of the schools from which they graduated into conversations.

When I was young, society was not so mobile and southerners, at least, did not see life as a progress. Education did not so much shape the future adult's success, social or financial, as it tidied appearance and spread plaster over the wallboard of character. What lay behind the plaster eventually seeped into daylight, tying the individual to family and delighting friends who traced anecdotal similarities to kinfolk three and four generations removed. Since people rarely escaped family and place to become achievements, achievement did not amount to as much as it does today. Instead of providing the exoskeleton of identity, achievement was the comparatively insubstantial fat of a moment. Because we are not now so much family or place, achievement and the accumulation of material things matter a great deal. Since society is convinced that education is a cure-all strengthening weakness and shaping not so much virtue as the capacity to garner wealth and position, teachers are subjected to pressures greater than those experienced by the people who taught me fifty years ago.

Assignments

Teachers often write me asking advice. After describing the lessons she assigned, a teacher in Massachusetts asked, "Are these writing assignments really meaningful or are they just stupid? Is it meaningful to have a high school sophomore write a character sketch of someone who has influenced her? Is it right to have them write four-and-five-paragraph essays on a short story or a novel they've read?" A teacher in New Jersey sent me the reading list for her high school's English Department and asked me to revise it, so that "it would be relevant and mean something to the students." Frequently a question is the excuse for a letter. Many of my correspondents are tired, "burned-out," as they put it. They have lost optimism and energy and write hoping I can supply some magical intellectual or spiritual elixir that will enable them to recapture what they recall as years of splendor in the classroom.

Questions about assignments are easy to answer. The good teacher makes the bad work, be the bad a system or an assignment. In the hands of a weak teacher a good system or assignment fails. Assignments themselves are only exercises and for the most part are artificial structures, dictated by necessity. Reactions to books often sprawl well beyond four-or-five-paragraph essays and probably also range outside good grammar and prose. Nevertheless students should not write thirty-page reactions to books. As much as appreciation, students must learn to shape and organize. Moreover the harried teacher has neither the time nor the energy to devote days to grading long papers. A good teacher will make the five-paragraph assignment work and benefit a student. In college, students write long papers about books, also artificial structures. After college criticism for most people shrinks to an appreciative phrase or two—a terrific read, a helluva story.

Occasionally I teach a student who has kept all the tests she ever took and all the papers she wrote. For such a student assignments become so meaningful they trivialize her days. Occasionally someone says that education teaches children to think. Certainly good lessons make students pause and ponder. Nevertheless, I think age teaches more than school. As people grow older, the thoughtful become aware of and shape the stories of their lives. Reading lists should always be broad enough to be inclusive. They should also be flexible. If a bright third-grader wants to spend her summer reading Dickens and none of Dickens's novels are on the list, let her do so. Lists should encourage and not proscribe.

In responding to letters from weary teachers, I think myself on surer ground. I tell them that they probably are not burned-out, just older. "You are no longer twenty-six and comparatively free from worry. A pipe has frozen in the basement. Shingles have blown off the roof. You have children, sick friends, and aging parents. You understand more than you did when university sent you newly minted into the classroom. What you now know about life makes you gloomy." I do not offer cure-alls. They are for the naive. I suggest what I have suggested throughout this book: that they wander books and landscapes. Amid goldenrod and milkweed, Shakespeare and petri dishes, they might, I write, escape worry for a moment and regain energy. They might be able to put aching school matters into some satisfactory but ultimately private perspective.

Unless one is teaching a specific skill, the content of a lesson sometimes does not matter so much as the rigor and the spirit with which it is taught. For me much of the controversy about the literary canon was misguided. Some books dubbed great by long appreciation strike me as dreadful, while the pages of others still seem crowned with ivy. You should teach some books that have endured time and have long garnered praise, but mix them with the new and with books you like. What is crucial is that you enjoy what you teach, that you find your reading list rich and thought-provoking. Educate yourself and become familiar with the controversies surrounding books or the canon, then follow your educated inclination.

By all means look at lists of books labeled "Developmentally Appropriate." Let the list hint and tease. Do not let it replace your judgment. What intrigues one child won't do for another. People often embrace the doctrinal because it spares them the labor, and the agony, of thought. Whenever I teach children's literature, students ask me to define a children's book. I always say, "A children's book is a book read by a child, be that book *Scuffy, the Tugboat, The House at Pooh Corner,* or *East of Eden.*" The answer satisfies the quicker students, being specific enough to function as a definition yet vague enough not to limit. Students who want life diagrammed like a sentence are not satisfied. If such students become teachers, their first days in the classroom will cause them great anxiety. If you meet such students in your classroom, go ahead and diagram reading for them. Forget yourself and do what they want done if it makes reading more attractive to and easier for them.

Much of what happens in a classroom cannot be predicted or planned for. Surprise and disappointment are part of the content of almost every lesson. Because numbers appear clearer than words on superficial examination, teachers write and ask me how challenging lessons should be. Frequently teachers instruct me to select a figure from one to ten, one being the easiest lesson, ten the most difficult. I do not answer the question directly, for the same reason I eschew defining a children's book. What challenges one child may not challenge another child. Despite teaching's usually focusing on a community of students—a grade, rather than an individual student—teachers should do their best to accommodate difference. For my part, however, I would rather err on the side of ease than on the side of difficulty. For nine years I read to my children. School forced me to stop. Teachers assigned so much homework that my children, who were conscientious students, did not have the leisure to listen to me read. Many assignments that superceded my reading smacked of busywork, making a poster for a book or drawing and coloring a map.

To be sure, a lack of homework frees children to be mischievous. Moreover parents often confuse the weight of homework with the quality of homework. To parents long assignments can make teachers appear responsible, people who are performing their duties conscientiously, people who know the importance of good study habits. On the other hand children ought to have freedom enough to educate themselves in part, even very young children. All many children need are suggestions. Because schools in Perth did not assign much homework, my children taught themselves, reading widely, sometimes according to plan, often according to whim. Because the children were accustomed to heavy assignments, the first time we were in Australia the lack of homework initially caused anxiety, and the children worried about falling behind friends in Connecticut. The anxiety soon vanished, however. Free just to be, rather than always struggling to become, the children relaxed into fun. They read and meandered, and on coming back to Connecticut they found they had not slipped behind. On the other hand freedom makes many children uneasy. They want to measure themselves and need a clear sense of accomplishment. Many children practically demand that they be measured by standards beyond the self, and if they are deprived of such standards they act up, concluding that they are not progressing. The teaching life is not easy. Even though you may want to give a few students space enough to educate themselves, you may not be able to do so. One of the best ways of controlling classes is by teaching and providing students with structure and firm goals, something that almost necessarily restricts freedom and undercuts individuality.

Abstraction

At the beginning of the university year in Western Australia, I wrote a short piece for "Insight," the local newspaper's educational supplement. I did not have space enough to ruminate or ponder the controversial or original. Instead I fertilized old chestnuts and covered them with a spread of story. I entitled the piece "Dorky," *dork* being slang for a person who does not belong to popular groups, usually an outsider, an odd person, sometimes inept, other times cranky. For my purpose a dork was an individual, the person who studied life and roamed far enough intellectually to be opinionated and have the courage to act. I concluded the article by urging new students, "Do well in your studies. Be an active member of the university. Learn to appreciate other people. Become tolerant, not of things that are intolerable but of different ways of living. Then dare to be a dork." The greatest risk of plans and systems is that they "privilege" the abstract and transform individuals into groups. They minimize the particular and can strip personality from an individual, all those edges that make us us. The parts of a class, the Johns and Sallys, are greater than the whole. Systems that reduce people to abstractions are dangerous. Once people become an abstract group, a "they," or "those people," then abuse comes easier. Abusing the individual is harder than abusing a group. Teachers see this demonstrated every year. Grading a big class, a lecture of two hundred students in which I don't know individuals, is easy. Because the students are strangers, grades are more fair than they are in smaller classes. I know the names of students in small classes. I know their histories. I know more than I want to know. I know things that disturb and things that make me laugh and shudder. A boy nurses a mother with multiple sclerosis. A girl works three jobs in order to pay for her schooling. Humanity affects the grades I give, tempering abstract fairness with kindness. Should what you know about a student's life influence a grade? Perhaps not, but it will, and its doing so is not something reprehensible but a sign of your humanity, of your refusal, maybe incapacity, to treat people as abstractions.

Life inhabits the particular. In speeches I mouth generalities. Invariably the small talk that follows a speech is more vital than the speech itself. After I talked in Perth one evening, teachers approached me. "For a man you aren't bad," a woman said. "I had a tough time in class today," a lively and comely young teacher said. "My knickers kept getting stuck in my bum, and I had to tweak them out." "You have a beautiful inner being," began a teacher who had embraced the new age. "I want to see your soul. Speak from the heart and reveal yourself." Another teacher handed me a note. "Read this later," she said. I read it on the way home. "Keep Seeking Yourself," the note said. "Shit, this is silly. I'm right here," I thought and tossed the note out the car window.

Teachers shouldn't waste time seeking themselves, but they should keep thinking. One of the most important points this book makes is that little is simple. In Western countries people set goals and try to solve problems. At day's end, though, life often seems out of joint, and doubt sweeps like fog across our minds obscuring accomplishment and leaving us feeling lost and befuddled. Maybe the Western emphasis on the individual is responsible for such feelings. Instead of stamping footprints in the sands of time, maybe life would be better lived if one sank anonymously into the soil itself, reaching a natural equilibrium, so much so that identity would be a symptom of imbalance. Instead of quantifying life in a series of measurements, wouldn't man and his host, the earth, fare better if societies celebrated harmonies, silences in which people floated contentedly and did not thrash toward achievement?

Competition

"Your students won't resent it if you give them A's," a teacher told me when I began teaching. Last fall, two days before I returned a midterm examination, a student asked for my office hours. "I want to know your office hours," he said, "so I can come by and complain about my grade. I deserve an A in this course." The boy made a B, and the day after receiving his paper he came to my office and complained. One hundred and seven students took the course. The girl who made the lowest grade in the class on the midterm also came to my office. I spent seventy-two minutes explaining how she could improve her work. I urged her to attend class and read the assignments, things she had not done. That afternoon when I returned home an e-mail from the girl greeted me. "I don't understand," she wrote, "why I didn't get a B. My friends got B's, and they didn't attend class, and I want you to know that you aren't fair."

Another girl retrieved a midterm after classes had ended for the semester. Commentary covered her blue book. She did not glance at the remarks. Instead she flipped to the final page, looked at the grade, and said, "This is unacceptable. You have to raise the grade." The class had taken the midterm the day before spring vacation. The day after vacation, March 26, I returned the tests. Every day until May 9, the last day of term, I carried the midterms to class. The girl had blown into my office like an ill wind. When I refused to change her grade, she complained to the head of the English Department. That night I told Vicki that I was so fed up with students that I thought I would retire. "Don't smash the lectern until tomorrow," she said. The next morning was sunny and I went for an amble. Bobolinks bounced across the field behind the old police station, and the girl vanished from mind.

In fact ill winds are not always troublesome. Harold cleaned the English Department where I once taught. He was a man addicted to high spirits and low living. While cleaning, particularly on Mondays, he would let fly rousers. One Monday Jonathan came into my office to complain about a grade. His papers were poor. Once I attempted to cushion the inevitable C by praising the first sentence of an essay. "This sentence," I said, "is quite good." "It ought to be," Jonathan responded. "I wrote it." Jonathan was just gnawing into his new complaint as well as my spirits when Harold went whistling past the door. "Surely," Jonathan said, "if you had thought at all when you read this paragraph, you would have . . ." Jonathan did not finish the sentence. A look of disgust swept across his face. "Good Lord," he exclaimed, then jerked his paper off my desk and left the office. A moment later I knew why he'd left. The ill wind boded well, and Jonathan never bothered me again.

Students often ask me to raise a grade, explaining that they need a higher mark in order to graduate. A friend once recounted that when a student who had earned a D asked for a C in his course, he said he would be glad to oblige. "But," my friend had said, "I am not going to give you a C. When I give a person a present, I want him to remember it. I am going to give you an A." "No," the student protested. "Don't give me an A. I didn't earn it. That would be terrible." When my friend insisted on the A, the student left his office, grade unraised. The story is good but it sounds apocryphal, the academic equivalent of the urban myth, a tale narratively akin to that of the babysitter, cruising along the shoulder of awareness, her fuel tank stoked with chemicals, who put the macaroni into the crib and the baby into the microwave.

Competition for grades is more intense today than when I was a student. Students and parents believe that entry to college and graduate school depends upon grades. Oddly the intense competition has to some degree lessened the importance of grades. The average of practically everyone who applies to the University of Connecticut to study English in graduate school is almost perfect. Grades are so high that I discount them. In undergraduate classes, however, the C is the contemporary equivalent of the old D-. Students who receive C's and who really deserve D's invariably complain, arguing that they deserved B's or A's. "Well, maybe not an A," as one girl put it, "but certainly an A-." The F, incidentally, is endangered, given only to the person who never comes to class and makes a zero on the examination. "Don't give F's," a dean told a friend. "If you give a student an F, he will take your class again. Give the student a D, and he will vanish. I view the D as the F cum laude."

The expression "it pays to pester" is as American as the land mine. In hopes of wearing teachers down and getting them to change their grades, a number of university students complain about every mark they receive other than an A. The deans know the students. I once attended a meeting in which several deans urged the faculty to resist pressure from students. The number of such students is growing. Pestering works. At semester's end, faculty are tired of tests, papers, and classes. Many faculty will change grades just to be left alone. The Internet has intensified complaint. Once upon a time students received grades six weeks after a term ended. By then the semester had almost drifted out of mind. Now grades are posted electronically within moments of having been turned in. When the professor gets home from his office, an e-mail complaint will greet him. Like everyone teachers are imperfect and make mistakes. When a student asks me to reexamine a paper, I do so carefully. If I think I've made a mistake I change the grade. I grade papers meticulously, how-ever, and rarely do I change grades. Never, though, do I lower a grade. I don't think it fair to penalize students who have real questions about papers and who want to learn to better their performances.

I always keep my office door open when I meet a student. Moreover I sit on the opposite side of the desk. Structure represses but it also supports order. Students can be aggressive. Some have tried to browbeat friends. I do not tolerate the unruly. If a student behaves badly in my office, something that happens very rarely, I don't react immediately. A day's wait contributes to perspective. Often something other than a grade provoked the behavior. Two days after a boy misbehaved, his father called me. "I just wanted to let you know," he said, "that my son won't be attending the rest of your class. He is in the Institute for Living [a sanatorium]. I am calling because he said you are his favorite teacher, the only person who cared for him, and he wanted you to know he would not be in class." If a student continues to behave badly and, for example, sends e-mails, I write him. In the letter I say that because of his "outrageous behavior" I can no longer meet him alone in my office. In the future, I write, any meeting with me must take place in the presence of a third party, a dean whom I name and whose address and phone number I provide in the letter. I also say that I have forwarded a copy of my letter and any correspondence he has sent me to the dean. So far that has always led to calm of mind, all passion spent.

Students who want to learn from tests stand out as do those who want only to nag teachers into giving them higher marks. Many students confuse work with achievement and demand to be rewarded for effort, not performance. Such students are accustomed to having effort rewarded in elementary and high school, a practice of which I approve but which ought to decrease as students approach the end of secondary school. All of us want to imagine that life rewards virtue, when rationally we know that just as often life rewards bad behavior. Still, truth can blight budding, and if you think a slight distortion will encourage and maybe lead to blossoms, then push a mark a little higher than it should otherwise be. Your students won't resent it. Neither will their parents. Maybe both will be encouraged.

Letter Eight: Pressure

DEAR TEACHER,

Having endured the slings and arrows of book reviewers for two decades, only rarely does unwarranted pestering bother me. My reaction to the girl's complaining about her grade after the last class was unusual. What irritates, however, is students' lack of style or planning. When I was in college, I rarely walked into a teacher's office. When I did enter an office I was prepared for conversation, just as I was prepared for examinations at the end of a semester. Mr. Ballard, the old boy who taught me philosophy at Sewanee, had aged beyond being able to distinguish a C paper from an A paper. Although I was the best student in the class, he gave me B's, a small matter but something that irked me. Early one morning before class I drank a stiff cup of coffee to get my brain percolating and went to his office. Declaring that one was going to major in philosophy pushed a grade up to B+. I began by saying I was going to major in philosophy, something I knew I would change as soon as the semester ended. To bump the big B into the little A required a smidgen more oil.

I wasn't sure exactly what to do next, but my tongue was greased. "Oh, I am so pleased you want to major in philosophy," Ballard said, beaming. "And by the way, what do you think of Aristotle?" Readiness was all. Inspiration sprang into words soft and creamy. "I like Aristotle just fine," I answered, "but Socrates has changed my life. You know Leo Parini, don't you?" Leo lived in my dormitory and was another temporary philosophy major. "Yes, indeed," the man answered, "a most perceptive student. I see a great deal of him." "Leo and I," I continued, "are roommates. At the beginning of the semester we didn't room together. We met in your course and became so interested in philosophy that we decided to room together in order to discuss your lectures. Every evening," I continued as Ballard sat across from me, puffing and swelling like a muffin soaked in margarine, "every evening we choose some controversial topic and debate it according to the Socratic method. To you, sir, we owe all our intellectual growth. You and your teaching have changed our lives. For the first time in our lives we are capable of thought."

"Oh, my, Pickering," Ballard began, almost teary, "your words overwhelm me. They make me glad I am a teacher. Sometimes, you know, teaching can be lonely and dispiriting." "Sir," I answered, leaning forward and laying my hand like a butter knife on the old boy's knee, "don't be dispirited. When you get down in the dumps, think of Leo and me and the hundreds of other students for whom you have made a lasting difference." "Bless you, Pickering, bless you," the old man answered. In class later that morning, he repeated my tale, omitting, thank the Lord, Leo's and my name. He said that in all his years of teaching no tribute had so touched him. At the end of the course I received an A. I never set foot in a philosophy class again and the next semester I became an English major. To get me to raise grades students have offered me all sorts of things, including cloth for suits, always with no success, but no one has ever offered me such a delightful story. If a student ever did serve up such a tale, I just might raise the grade.

Among the papers Amanda kept as memorabilia from her teaching days were notes from parents. Many explained why children had missed school. Kelly missed school on Tuesday, his mother said, because "he had bands put on his teeth Monday and his mouth was *very* sore." Preston, another mother wrote, "has a cold and feels bad, so I let him stay at home yesterday. If you think he is too droopy to be at school today, just send him home. I think he probably spread all the germs Monday and might as well attend today, in case of learning something." An auditorium of parents worried about grades. "Does Pamela concentrate in class when you are explaining how to do math?" a mother asked. "Apparently she's not on or something. If she's not listening maybe a firmer hand would help from you as from me. Her grades are terrible." "Dear Mrs. Pickering," another parent wrote. "I am grateful for Marcia's Arithmetic grade. She was very pleased when she was able to stay with you after school, and it seems to do wonders for her. I hope that you will be able to help her more these next six weeks after school."

Grade pressure has increased in multiples since the 1960s. In fact many parents hurry children through childhood so that they will get a mind or a leg up on their companions. Summers are lost in intense study and "intenser" play. Children who can hardly run are thrown into soccer camp. Other children go to computer camp. Fifth-graders attend football camp. You will not be able to escape the ratcheting up of pressure and expectation. No matter your efforts to defuse competition, you will fail. In the twelve years my three children attended local schools, I went to only one parent-teacher conference, and that was when Francis began middle school. I canceled all the other conferences. In hopes of deflating pressure, I did not look at report cards on the days children brought them home. Eventually I read the cards because the children were proud of their marks and wanted to be praised. But as soon as Vicki and I glanced at the cards we buried them out of sight. Yet all my children have said I am the most intense, competitive person they have ever met. They have accused me of putting immense pressure on them to get good grades. "You may not have said anything, but that just made it worse. We knew what you wanted." The statement smacks of the invisible-cat argument. One man points to a chair and says, "There is an invisible cat in that chair." The other man answers, "The chair is empty. I don't see a cat." "That just proves my point," the first man replies. "You don't see the cat because it is invisible."

No matter what they thought I did or did not do, the children felt under pressure to make high marks, most of the pressure inhaled from the air around them, coming from the tenor of a society that forever ranks and rates and does not let children relax and play enough because it defines them as lists of accomplishments. Paradoxically as grades have increased in importance, many high schools have abolished valedictorians and salutatorians and have substituted percentage groupings for rank. Although this may appear to be "dumbing down," it is in fact "academic upping." Schools have adopted the measures because increasing numbers of parents think grades increasingly significant and believe it better for college applications if their children appear in a top percentile rather than ranked tenth, twelfth, or twenty-second. Getting rid of the valedictorian and salutatorian penalizes only two students while enabling a group of students to share "top" honors.

In Australia the wonderful teacher who taught Eliza during the second half of our first year in Perth wrote a note to Eliza. Around the note she put seventeen stickers, among others, a pink horse, a yellow and blue butterfly, a blue whale, and two teddy bears sliding down a rainbow. On the card she wrote, "Remember, it's okay not to be perfect all the time." Unfortunately, we didn't stay in Australia. At the beginning of her junior year, Eliza took the College Board Examinations. She made 760 in both math and English. She was upset, and shortly after she'd received the results I found her on the Internet booking the tests again. "I have to get 800s," she said. "No, you don't," I said and broke the telephone connection. "Well," she said, "I will have to make 800s on the SAT IIs." "You don't," I said. "But I will," she said. "The brothers did, and I have to also."

Prepare yourself for the pressures parents, especially middle-class parents, will put upon you and their children. Boys who "broke" the honor code at MBA usually did so not to improve a grade so much as to satisfy a parent and thus make home more bearable. Fomenting competition and its accompanying pressure are also big money earners. Throughout elementary and high school, my children received flyers advertising summer programs, which would, if not guarantee them admission into top colleges, give them a handhold in the Ivy. Last year I gave a keynote talk at a one-day conference sponsored by the Johns Hopkins University Center for Talented Youth. The audience consisted of three hundred people: seventh- and eighth-graders and their parents.

In the 1950s book companies sold encyclopedias to lower-middle-class parents. Most of the parents had not attended college, and salesmen claimed the books would boost children to the heads of their classes, ultimately enabling them to enroll in college. Because of growing affluence, not encyclopedias, the children attended college. Now solidly middle class, those children themselves have become parents. To these people Johns Hopkins marketed programs for "Talented Youth," appealing to a hope similar to that which book companies had made their pitch fifty years earlier. Instead of going to their alma maters, colleges down the road, parents now imagined their babies attending an Ivy League school or at least a distinguished state university. Nowadays the bait of flattering hope always hooks parents. At the conference several parents requested certificates that would testify to their children's participation and which could be used in applications to college—five or six years later!

Parents often write me not because they care what I think, but in order to enlist me in putting pressure on a child's teacher. In replies I avoid saying anything that could be used to criticize a child's teacher. Late one winter a man wrote from Delaware, asking me to assess a poem written by his daughter, an eighth-grader. The girl had written the poem one morning during math class. Later that day she showed the poem to her English teacher. When the teacher did not praise the poem effusively, or so the father recounted, the girl was upset. "Please be as objective as you can and let her know what you think about her poem," the father said, then added a sentence meant to undercut objectivity. "She needs your support at this time." Entitled "Sad," the poem began, "Sad tree. Sad house. / Spinning flowers in my life." The remaining ten lines did not contribute much more to the poem.

That afternoon I wrote the girl. "Your father sent me a copy of your poem 'Sad.' You have a nice lyric sense, and the piece is soft and gentle," I began. "But I will tell you what I tell students at the university. You have made a beginning, but you must push on." I urged the girl to read poetry and suggested several collections. "Writing," I said, "does not come easily. My friends who publish poetry sometimes revise their poems thirty or forty times. Poetry results more from work—hard, slogging work—than from inspiration." Lastly, I wished the girl good luck and then described something silly I did on the athletic rather than the poetic field when I was her age. Because the letter did not undercut his daughter's English teacher, the father was disappointed and wrote me back angrily. He said I would not recognize a good poem if I saw one, giving the lie to his plea for objectivity. He and his daughter agreed that I was no longer the teacher depicted in *Dead*

Poets Society. "You have lost the ability to inspire." I marveled at the letter then tossed it into the recycle can. Parents will say dreadful things to you. Do not let them burrow under the skin and get into your bloodstream. If you have to respond, go into your office alone, shut the door, and quote Tennessee Williams, preferably a terse, ripe phrase, something like "Screw you" or "Kiss my ass." Afterward open your door, chuckle, step into the hall, and smile like the sunrise.

A Few Platitudes

One Friday in Australia Eliza and I went to the local library. Tacked to a board was a flyer advertising a lecture entitled, "How to Prevent Aging." "There is only one sure way to prevent aging," I said to the librarian. "What's that?" she said, stamping books and not paying much attention to my statement. "Death," I barked. "What?" she said, looking up and pushing away from her desk. "Death," I repeated, stepping closer. "Death is the only certain cure for aging. Only fools will attend the lecture." "Daddy," Eliza said later, "you frightened that nice woman." "Good," I said, "truth disturbs."

Of course I should have kept my mouth shut. Your success may depend as much upon what you don't say as what you do say. Fictions thrive everywhere but they do especially well in school environments. "Take the humbug out of life," Josh Billings, the nineteenth-century humorist, said, "and you won't have much left to do business with." No matter what their occupations, people talk and write conventionally, relying upon words and phrases that they haven't analyzed critically. If you persist in throwing them to the intellectual mat, you will soon be thought a crank. Still, to keep your mind sharp, you must ponder phrases commonly bandied about in educational discussions. Of course common phrases function as intellectual shorthand. The problem is that they distort and shortchange thought. Tacked to a bulletin board in the classroom in which I taught this fall was a poster. Printed on the poster in big black letters was the command TEACH THE WHOLE CHILD. Beneath the imperative someone, resembling me, at least intellectually, had written, "except the private parts."

The phrase "role model" seems to be as popular among educators as the Comedy Central channel is among teenagers. Only the unexamined life is exemplary. No life can stand scrutiny and interpretation, this last usually bent by biographers in order to startle and thus sell books. In part "role model" is just an example gone uptown and dressed in fancy duds. Yet it is different, raising the image, say, of a toy train, each part smaller than the original, as children are smaller than adults, but still in scale. Implied in the celebration of role model is the assertion that if children copy adults meticulously they can, if not become those adults, then at least succeed to the same degree. The implication, of course, is a lie. Moreover, the concept itself is probably a fiction and, like so many fictions, one imposed paternalistically by the well meaning upon the poor and deprived, of whose actual lives the good intentioned usually know little. I have never met a student who modeled her life on that of another person. By all means describe good examples, but do not assume that example will change behavior.

Bad example or the "unrole model" can terrify and often changes people quicker than good example. Moreover copying good example does not necessarily bring happy results. In "His Little Hatchet," Petroleum V. Nasby, the nineteenth-century American wit, described the results of mimicking good example. "I commenced being good at a very early age and built myself up on the best models," Nasby wrote. "I was yet an infant when I read the affecting story of the hacking down of the cherry tree by George Washington, and his manly statement to his father that he could not tell a lie. I read the story and it filled me with a desire to surpass him. I was not going to let any such a boy as George Washington, even if he did afterwards get to be President, excel me in the moralities." Nasby then proceeded to chop down his father's most valuable cherry tree. After felling the tree, he went Washington one better and dug up the roots, "so that by no means could the variety be preserved." Nasby eagerly anticipated confessing and being "wept over and forgiven" because of his "extreme truthfulness." The plan failed. "I was very much like George Washington, but the trouble was that my father didn't resemble George Washington's father." On being asked, "Did you chop down the cherry tree?" Nasby responded, "Father I cannot tell a lie. I did it with my little hatchet." Nasby then struck "the proper attitude for the old gentleman to shed tears on me." Alas, his father said that "he had rather I told a thousand lies than to have cut down that particular tree, and he whipped me until I was in an exasperated rawness."

Unlike role model, example is real. "My family was poor. My parents didn't read, and there were few books in the house when I was growing up," a friend told me. "I liked reading and checked books out of the school library, but I didn't think about teaching until the sixth grade. The man who taught the sixth grade held books delicately and turned pages carefully. He told the class that books mattered, and he read us stories and poetry. One day while listening to him read and watching him turn pages, I thought, 'This is what I am going to do. I'm going to teach.'"

You should be your students' best example. Show them that you enjoy teaching and that what you teach matters. Little things will contribute to your success as an example. For instance, how students address you matters. You are not Emma or Raymond. You are a teacher. You are Miss Johnson, Mrs. Ratcliffe, Ms. Catlin, Mr. Griffin, and Coach Garthright. Titles preserve and elevate. Certainly formality can inhibit and imprison. Yet in classrooms, which inevitably spiral toward chaos, they help preserve order. They serve as drags on untoward recklessness. They help define you as someone important, a person worth listening to and obeying.

Another phrase that has been used past the threadbare stage is "learning experience." The phrase offers false consolation and is symptomatic of people's fierce determination to be positive and optimistic and thus frees them from scrutinizing living. Generally people undergo something dreadful. On recovering they say,

"While it was going on, it was terrible. But the ordeal was a learning experience. I'm a better person for it. Now that it is over, I am thankful for the experience." Not long ago Hoben Donkin met Floyd Templeton outside Read's drugstore in Carthage. "Floyd," Hoben said, "I haven't seen you for the longest time. How've you been?" "Not so well," Floyd answered. "Last summer I disturbed a bear eating blackberries." "Oh, my Lord," Hoben said. "What happened?" "The bear chased me," Floyd said. "Although I ran as fast as I could, he caught me, and before I had a chance to introduce myself, he killed me and ate me." "That's the worst thing I've ever heard," Hoben said. "I'm so sorry." "Well, thank you," Floyd answered. "It wasn't pleasant, but I learned a lot from the experience, and if I weren't dead, I could put it to good use." "I bet you could. You're just the man for it. Nobody could do better. I'm really sorry you died," Hoben said somberly. "Thanks for that, too," Floyd said. "I appreciate your sympathy and concern."

Dream and unwarranted expectation flourish in a mobile society. Although many Americans are born in peonage, they are not legally bound to it. Only imagination limits what Americans think they or, in the case of schools, their children can accomplish. When the shell of expectation shatters and people's hopes for themselves prove rotten, they still can imagine their children breaking free from hard circumstances and soaring fully fledged over the impossible. Most Americans see life as linear and upward, a progress in which people, particularly children, stride toward secular achievement, growing by overcoming challenges. In this vision education is the handmaiden of success. When a child reaches a barrier, education extends a hand. The classroom would be different if Americans saw life as circular. Then perhaps education would not stress mastery as much as appreciation, accomplishment more than joy.

Some years ago a student interviewed me for an assignment. What aspects of my life, she asked, had changed during the past five years. I explained that little had changed. Unlike earlier hunks of time during which children were born and parents died, when dreams and ambition fermented, recent years had stretched flat, calm, and happy. "The only change that the past five years has brought to my life," I said, "is the wonderful absence of change." In the platitudinous view of life as a continuing progress, stasis is failure. My answer disturbed the student. "I'm supposed to talk about change and challenge," she said. "I'll have to interview someone else." Teachers know that yearly grade reports that show progress from, say, 72 to 76 or 82 to 88 satisfy parents and administrators.

No matter how good they are, school systems are pressured to "improve," or if not really improve then adopt changes that give the illusion of improvement and, in another wearying phrase, of "adapting to changing times." By all means try different methods. Work and try to better your teaching, but be aware that in education life can be circular; today's startling improvement may be a reworking of something done twenty years ago, then dropped and forgotten. Still, dry bones may live just because they appear unfamiliar. Nothing, though, as I keep pointing out, is simple. Although dry bones may invigorate classes, they may also kill, especially when politicians package them as a return to the basics, usually as an excuse to cut education budgets, "frills," they invariably say. The truth is that many teachers teach only the basics. Not only can their schools not afford frills but their students are ill prepared for anything other than basics. Alas, these are just the students who might benefit greatly from frills, inessentials that break the sad tenor of their lives. Instead of serving these students an impoverished low-calorie diet of basics, schools might better serve community by dishing out frills, high culture that might startle and awaken.

No one escapes generalities studded with words like *challenge* and *growth*. Educators are particularly susceptible to them because such platitudes justify their existence. If people stopped believing or paying lip service to the idea that education shaped adults, schools and universities would close and the economy would collapse. Because my son Francis did well on the PSATs, a sort of preliminary college entrance examination taken by juniors in high school, a foundation invited him to apply for a summer fellowship, six weeks spent at Kenyon or Cornell discussing identity. Applicants were instructed to write short essays, the topics the stuff of the old inspirational game, one "on a conflict you have faced and attempted to resolve," another evaluating a book "read outside of class."

Francis was an amiable boy who slipped seamlessly in and through diverse groups, avoiding conflict. Consequently I sought the advice of my friend Josh. Josh had no patience for the sentimentality the application seemed to elicit. "Francis should write,"

Josh suggested, "that for years a blond boy bullied me. This fall, however, I took a course in conflict resolution. The class made all the difference and taught me how to resolve quarrels. For a final project at the end of term I borrowed an iron bar from shop and hammered the bully's wrists through his elbows into his shoulder blades. Not only did I get an A+ for the course, but no one has bothered me since. In fact swarms of sissies admire me, and namby-pambies dog my every footstep."

The changes that will affect your room most will be bells and whistles, the stuff of technology. You will attend teaching institutes that will explain the benefits of technology, and if you are enthusiastic about what you learn, the knowledge will better your class. What no teaching institute has ever done is dissect personality and come up with a recipe for an ideal teacher. Good teachers are too various. Institutes can tinker and adorn. They can film your class and discover flaw and irritating mannerism, something potentially valuable. The man who taught my freshman math class suffered from tics. One day in a fifty-minute period he said "all right" fifty-five times and cleared his throat one hundred and twenty-one times.

I always got to class before the teacher arrived. The next class period I did not go straight to my desk. Instead I stood in front of the blackboard and imitated the teacher, clearing my throat and repeating "all right." Although spirited, my performance was not a success. I did not know that the man's wife was in the class. As a result my grade plummeted, my final mark determined not by tests but by retribution, not exactly fair but something I accepted as just. I learned a lesson. I did not stop imitating teachers but, before I did so, I made sure that no wives, husbands, children, lovers, or close friends were in the room. My performance having occurred before classes were filmed, so I suspect the teacher learned more than I did. Certainly during the rest of the term, the number of "all rights" and throat clearings decreased considerably. In fact I did the man such a service that if I remembered his name, I would e-mail him and demand a higher grade. I would not go so far, however, as to harangue him if he now resides in a nursing home.

All the institutes, seminars, symposia, and faculty improvement days you attend can be useful. You will learn small things. In addition such days provide opportunities to chat with your colleagues and to meet people. Much that you learn will be indirect, the stuff of relaxed conversation, table talk, not words determined by or shaped for a seminar room. As life thrives along fence rows and the edges of a cornfield, not in the field itself, so you may benefit more from doings surrounding a lecture than from the lecture itself. I am often asked to give motivational speeches. Occasionally I oblige, not because I have a mission but because I have to pay tuition. More often than not, however, I don't speak. Sometimes when I refuse to speak I tell the truth, and although my wallet is not flush I feel better about myself.

"In June," a woman wrote me when we lived in Australia, "Price Waterhouse of Malaysia is sponsoring a management conference in Perth. One hundred and twenty account executives are flying from Kuala Lumpur. They will spend two days at the

Burswood Resort. During mornings and afternoons they will attend lectures. We would like you to be one of our facilitators." I met the woman downtown. "Workshops at the conference," she said, "will explain the firm's new mission. We want managers to have a vision and to understand the firm's values." She handed me a sheet of "objectives." They were trite, the sorts of words that you will read many times during your career and that instead of awakening and invigorating will rock you to sleep. "By the end of the workshop," participants will "be convinced of the power of vision and of the importance of values." They will "understand what change is and why it is both necessary and vital." They will "be able to manage themselves in an environment of change and will feel positive about it." Moreover they will "be able to influence their subordinates so that the latter are equally receptive to change and feel motivated, excited, and positive about the prospects of introducing the firm's vision, mission, and values."

Only the Second Coming could affect such miraculous changes. In companies in which turnover of employees is rapid, alas, including schools, motivational speeches are popular, one "human resource director" told me, forming part of "rest and recreation days." At best the speeches resemble Grandmother's remedy for a cold: a teaspoon of sugar in a shot of bourbon. Sweet and palatable, a talk may intoxicate for a moment and actually clear worry from the head for an hour. By the end of a morning, however, the congestion of chore and responsibility invariably return to plug the day. Nevertheless use your time around the talk well. Don't schedule every moment, but meander and talk to strangers. You may learn a lot. "We do not know today whether we are busy or idle," Emerson wrote in "Experience." "In times when we thought ourselves indolent, we have afterwards discovered that much was accomplished."

"Instead of having them listen to me," I told the woman, "why don't you order your managers to swim through a pool of strawberry ice cream? The ice cream will cost less, and the managers will never forget the experience." Despite my suggestion, maybe because of it, the woman asked me to send her a proposal for the conference. I do not know whether life is circular or not. I do know that long periods of stasis exist, especially intellectual periods. Instead of a proposal I wrote the woman a letter. Although abbreviated, the contents of the letter resemble things I have written to you. I urged the woman to flesh out *vision* and *mission*. For most people, I said, Price Waterhouse is a financial institution, a report printed on glossy paper sent to shareholders or a tall building with opaque windows staring over busy streets. "Did the company want to appear humane?" I asked. In the United States many corporations attempted to change their public images, if not their substance, by seeming to become eco-friendly, making contributions to environmental organizations. Did mission extend beyond sloganeering and involve more than platitudes or "showcasing" glitzy programs depicting Price Waterhouse as a responsible and concerned corporation? Most people believe accounting hard and statistical, the poetry of numbers cacophonous, not rising through quatrains singing but instead sinking dead against a bottom line. Did mission imply that employees would be urged to stray outside asset and liability columns?

Beyond the page, I said, life was not clear. Even the best-kept books rarely balanced. My letter was commonsensical plain fare. "If you really want employees to become more creative and enthusiastic, encourage them to enrich their lives. The living room opens into the office. Private life influences public life. The concerns of home often determine both the manner in which an employee accomplishes tasks and the satisfaction he finds in a job." At conferences, I wrote, pleasure was more important than learning. "Avoid a rigorous course of meetings; too many lectures tire people and drain the spirit."

What I suggested for accountants is probably true for teachers. I ended by saying I thought that sending employees to Burswood Resort and Casino was a mistake. "For the person who loses a bankbook of money gambling, the conference will be a failure, no matter who speaks. The next time Price Waterhouse sends accountants to Western Australia bundle them off to Rottnest Island [a small island near Perth] for a long weekend. Hire bicycles and prepare picnic lunches for them. Urge them to spend days exploring the island. Don't try to accomplish much. Ideas blend nicely with coffee after breakfast and dessert after dinner. They don't go down so well during the rest of the day. No matter the cook stirring the lesson, ideas curdle by ten-thirty in the morning and nine-thirty at night."

Metaphors may shape reality even if they are raised upon distortion. Without government aid, tax breaks, and subsidies of all hues, many corporations would fold. That reality aside, however, school administrators are fond of proclaiming that education is becoming more efficient and more businesslike. So far as I know, no school system in Connecticut has saved money by retrenching, say, getting rid of the fifth and tenth grades, or by outsourcing, sending teachers to Mexico or Indonesia where salaries and health benefits are lower. Schools, however, have embraced the word *accountability*. Unfortunately the word doesn't apply to education, many of whose most valuable results are not quantifiable. Indeed the word does not apply to ballet, art, raising a child, eggnog, or Christmas Eve. The word strips away much that really counts in life, leaving people with the illusion of being functional and creating a dangerously dysfunctional state of mind. To people deceived by rote and definition, the truly functional appear to be ditherers. That aside, however, as teachers you will be called to account for all sorts of unaccountable things, not just pencils on your desk or paper clips in your drawer.

My advice is to temporize. Write statements that show you are monitoring yourself and that reveal you are improving. Respond to evaluation with a display of good feeling and gratitude. Create categories and slots that you can cram with statistics: students taught, papers assigned, conferences held, meetings attended, the number of students you have exposed to "life experiences," pages of workbooks finished, on and on. You know that teaching is both art and gift. Others do not, so give them what they expect in order to prevent them from interfering and undermining your classes. Also popular among folks in the managerial class is the word *narrative*. If asked to evaluate yourself, call what you write a narrative. Writing a narrative is simple. Good narratives resemble positive, heart-wrenching stories like those published in *Reader's Digest*. Describe an upward awakening progress. Spangle the account with superlatives; adorn it with epiphanies and cries of "eureka" and "excelsior"; then get on with teaching and living.

I know this advice may appear cynical. I prefer to think it practical, reflecting a hardheaded, product-oriented, business methodology. Much that you will be asked to do will strike you as busywork. Do it without fretting and sapping energy. Because they are bigger than schools, universities offer more opportunities to scoot around work. Several years ago an administrator got the notion that not enough classes were being taught early in the morning. The administrator ordered department heads to study recent schedules and compile a report detailing percentages of courses offered at each hour during the academic day. Even with a computer the task was large. "How long did the report take?" I asked B.G., head of one of the biggest departments on campus. "Eighteen minutes," he said. "I called the administrator's office and asked what percentages he thought ideal for the various hours of the day. Afterward I wrote my report bettering the ideals for every hour." "You didn't look at a single schedule?" I said. "Of course not," B.G. answered. "I had better things to do. A year later at a meeting of department heads, I asked about the reports. No one in administration had ever looked at them."

After you have taught for a year or so, you will find yourself on committees. If you retreat into silence, work will be piled upon you. The best way to insure that a committee does not absorb all your free time is to take charge. Then you can parcel out duties. If a report must be written, ask everyone on the committee for written contributions then write the report yourself. Before submitting the report to the powers who think that they be, give everyone on the committee a copy of your report and again ask for suggestions in writing. If you can prevent additional meetings, do so. Incorporate sane suggestions into the final report. Ditch the others tactfully. I always send members of the committee notes telling them which suggestions of theirs I used and which I did not use. I explain that although I thought all their suggestions bright other members of the committee held differing opinions. I explain that in pages other members of the committee sent me they specifically stated that we should avoid the matters I removed from the final report. Of course I received no such responses. This technique works, I must warn you, only if committees are large and the members are not good friends. Moreover the committee must be insignificant as most happily are.

Editing a journal taught me the technique. After receiving a manuscript, many academic journals send the manuscript to outside readers. Not only is postage expensive but tracking manuscripts is onerous. Readers are lazy. They lose manuscripts and often take an unconscionable amount of time to read even a short essay. As a result editors waste afternoons writing letters, both pushing readers to read and apologizing to potential contributors. When I edited, I read the manuscripts myself and made all decisions concerning acceptance or rejection. I wrote a personal letter to each person who submitted a manuscript. If I rejected the manuscript, I found something in it to praise. Then I quoted the reader's report, the report, of course, a fiction. I usually said, "Our reader states." I went on to write "she thinks," after which I wrote, "not a contention with which I wholeheartedly agree but one which you might consider." Because academics hesitate to criticize women as strongly as they do men, I made my readers female.

Sometime during your career you will be asked to mentor new teachers, that is, help them and watch over them. Unless new teachers stumble badly and lose control of themselves or their classes, probably the best things you can do are to act concerned and be ready to advise. Chat with new teachers. If asked, make suggestions, but do not legislate and smother. Years ago when I first taught, two colleagues visited my classes. The first was an energetic man who paced his classroom, shouting, waving his arms, and even falling to the floor. The second was retiring and mild, so soft-spoken that I could hardly understand him. "Your class was very good," the first man told me, "but you need to be more energetic. Perhaps you should shout occasionally. Pound the blackboard. That will keep the sleepy alert." "I liked your class," the second man said, "but at times theatricality distracted from the lesson. The best way to teach is sitting down. Think of your desk as a muffler that prevents unseemly exertion and softens the approach to learning." Each man thought the best way to teach was the way he himself taught, not a bad lesson for me to learn. Don't, then, impose yourself upon new teachers. Still, be ready to help. Have lunch with new teachers occasionally. Suggest something new teachers can read, not necessarily this book but books about schooling and then, if you really want to help them get through days, and nights, a shelf of good mysteries. If, on the other hand, teachers whom you are mentoring treat you as a lactator and practically milk you dry with questions, you might suggest that they read time-consuming, complicated books, *Middlemarch,* for example. "I am curious about what you will think about *War and Peace,*" you might say. "When you finish the book, we will meet again."

Letter Nine: Requirements

DEAR TEACHER,

In this section I am going to talk about courses. To succeed in high school and most colleges today one must conform. Students who want to attend university buckle themselves to the "college track" and mechanically chug through requirements, no matter their inclinations or desires: four years of English and math, three of science, three of a foreign language, three of history and social studies, et cetera. Occasionally a newspaper describes the success of a child homeschooled, fostering the fiction that society and the educational system value quirky independence.

I am a Luddite. If given the chance I would shatter many of the educational frames confining thought and life. Of course children must learn skills, especially in elementary and high school. What skills these are varies according to age, time, and place. Moreover elementary and high schools have to limit choice because they cannot afford a huge range of courses. Still, requirements ought to be looser, particularly in college. Colleges should abolish general requirements. One course does not a historian make. Two diversity courses will not make a person tolerant and caring. If a child despises math, why must he take three math courses in college? On the other hand, if he loves math why not let him take all math courses? Proportionately a course in ecology and evolutionary biology probably turns out as many humanists as does English. In college give students direction, direction, and direction, but let them follow inclination, expedience, and interest. I think everyone should know a second language, but not everyone should be forced to learn a second language. It is not important for everyone to write well. Many presidents have been poor writers. When facing paper George Washington was ham-fisted. Let people who want to write well take composition classes. If people reach forty and suddenly regret lost opportunities, let them reeducate themselves. Instead of behaving egomaniacally and trying to impose compensatory requirements upon the educational system, let them suggest and warn. Let their new studies serve as examples. Let them teach and lead.

Changing established requirements is difficult. Three years ago the faculty senate at the university set about reducing general education requirements, that is, specific courses required for graduation in addition to a student's major. Some schools label such courses distribution requirements. The senate failed. Oddly, and unreasonably from my point of view, people who dislike and perform poorly in math must take one more course than students who are adept at math, the course being a "get-up-to-speed" elementary course that doesn't count toward graduation. Why should students who don't like a subject and find it difficult be compelled to spend more time studying that subject than other students? Shouldn't students who dislike math be allowed to take two courses rather than four? Perhaps universities should encourage such students to skip math all together and use that course time to explore the unfamiliar in hopes of unearthing dormant talents or of discovering new interests.

What applies to math also applies to English studies, particularly composition. As I noted earlier, being able to write well is not a qualification for being president either of the United States or of a major university. Writing poorly does not exclude a person from the pleasures of the bed- or boardroom. Writing courses clog the college curriculum. The subject is a gold mine for textbook publishers. Maybe someday I'll cash in on the fad for handbooks on writing, combining writing with other fashionable concerns, calling my book something like *The Nine-Step Process to Lasting Repentance, Good Prose, and Alcohol-and-Drug-Free Living.*

I teach writing. I don't use a book. During the semester each of my twenty students writes twelve essays for me, one a week, each essay accompanied by two rough drafts. By term's end the writing of most students has improved. Some members of the class will continue to write better during the next semester. Others won't take English again, and their writing will deteriorate. "I wanted you to know that I got into business school," a boy told me this fall. "The application required an essay. I haven't written much recently, so I submitted an essay I wrote for you four years ago. That did the trick. What do you think?" "Super," I said, the word a faucet squeezing off thought.

Writing is not as important as schools maintain. The poorest scribbler in my composition class can compose an effective love letter or order an air conditioner from Wal-Mart. Justifications for writing courses are usually shaky. "A person who writes clearly thinks clearly," a friend said recently. No, no, no—the person who writes clearly writes clearly. That is all that can be said. Thought is another and more complex matter. Schools preach the virtues of clarity. Obscurity is just as virtuous. While clarity is often damned by being associated with simplicity and superficiality, obscurity is celebrated by being associated with profundity. If you want to be thought profound, write obscurely and appear serious in public. Laugh only in private.

Often success depends upon avoiding clarity. Suppose a modern Juliet wrote her Romeo an e-mail in which she asked, "Dost thou love me?" Further, suppose Romeo loved bedding Juliet but not Juliet herself. And suppose, there being no other bit of the nifty on his radar, that Romeo wanted to continue doubling himself with Juliet. His reply might read like the following. "Dearest Moonbeam, how could you ask if I love you? Your lips are riper than cherries bussed by the sun. Your eyes flutter like bluebirds. Your nose is an ivory rudder turning the golden galleon of your visage. Your hair sparkles in the breeze like a host of wildflowers, a honeyed chorus of bees fiddling around them. Your behind resembles a gigantic watermelon, rose-red and ripe and luscious, and your toes are as soft and munchable as avocados [well, perhaps these last two comparisons are beyond the composition skills of youth]. Dearest, dearest Pooh Bear of my Heart, how could you doubt my love?"

Again what a teacher thinks outside class does not necessarily influence assignments. I demand clear prose. To this end I urge students to write short, declarative sentences, even though complexity roils my thought into long fragments. Although you should question the emphasis education places upon writing, you should beat drum and desk for clarity and simplicity in your classes. Indeed, lean on weary, superficial justifications. "You won't know what you think until you write your thoughts down," I sometimes say, crossing my fingers behind my back. More important, try your hand at writing. The effort may teach you a lot. Write pieces and submit them for publication. Where you send them does not matter much. Don't be discouraged by rejection. Consider the submission process a game. When I began mailing essays to magazines, I kept track of my "batting average," in other words, the acceptance rate. For years I was a journeyman, good in the field or classroom but not a hitter, batting .100 to .200, that is, about one or two acceptances for every ten pieces submitted. Actually I'm not much of a stickman today. I just write more. As a result my "in-journal percentage" appears higher at first glance than it really is.

I want now to suggest a course or two that I wish were offered. Wishes are not prescriptions, however. I encourage all students to learn at least one foreign language. If I could legislate such learning, though, I would not. I'd harangue, cajole, even beg, but I would not legislate, at least not in college. In high school teachers can and should steer students, herd them, more so than teachers do in college. Teach your students to read and think critically. Teach them mathematics. Encourage them to study the world surrounding them, be that world past or present. Awaken interests. Do not, though, make the mistake of seeing your classroom as a gathering of equals. You are the teacher because you have things to give students that they cannot give themselves. If you undervalue yourself and your difference from students, you will lose respect and your class. Teenagers quickly recognize the stink of false humility. Be confident enough to lead, even though you may wander down a wrong fork now and then.

Never forget that you are a leader. Help students. Lead them to and through learning. Be friendly. But do not try to seduce them into learning by pretending to relate to them. Dress appropriately. Schools send children home for inappropriate dress. Sometimes faculty should be put on the early bus. Cultivate an appropriate informality. This does not mean you must dress drably or look like a sartorial clone of Gap or L.L.Bean. If purple is your favorite color, wear it every day. Pleasant oddities appeal to children. If you wear purple every day, they will think you kooky and perhaps like you the more for it. Appropriate dress is matter of decorum more than a rule of taste. What is appropriate in one classroom or school may not be suitable in other schools and classrooms. Neckties go better with English literature than they do science labs, where they can be dangerous. A lumberjack outfit goes better with Thoreau than with Jane Austen. By all means dress according to inclination, rather inclination tempered by common sense. Study the clothes of colleagues. Find a mean between the undressed who resemble and often behave like hairballs and the overdressed whose flashy attire detracts from class.

Writing about clothes is priggish. What teachers wear, though, sometimes startles. A teaching assistant at the university routinely wears tight blue jeans, which slip so far off her hips that people behind her notice the top of her thong. Instead of describing the sight from the front, I am going to behave cowardly and quote a female professor, a woman given to strong, truthful statements. "Good Lord, Sam," she said. "I've never seen such undress in a classroom. I feel so sorry for that girl's male students. How dreadful it must be to suffer an erection for fifty minutes three times a week! Boys will learn nothing in that class. Sexual excitement and thought are not compatible."

In truth poems that link thought and passion swell anthologies. Of course when authors composed such poetry they sat in their studies, strapped to their desks by chastity belts of books and pens, only their imaginations free to wander wantonly. Be aware, however, that clothes affect young males and select your dress accordingly. For Carl the most memorable day of his tenure in middle school occurred in sixth grade when a substitute taught his class. Ms. Horne, the substitute, was a large woman who wore loose-fitting dresses. Carl sat in the front row of class. When Ms. Horne leaned over him to help him solve a math problem, her amplitude became apparent. As a result Carl suffered an inconvenience, the first time, he recounted, that such a thing had bothered him in school. The sight remained vibrant in his mind for some time. "With all my passion directed toward Ms. Horne," he said, "I paid little attention to the developing girls around me. All the gossip about training bras and talk about hitting the hormone wall awakened the sexuality of my peers. I never mentioned my 'crush' on Ms. Horne for fear of being ostracized. When the subject of girls came up, I always pretended to care about Erin's rear or Sarah's face. While the rest of my friends talked about girls, I thought about a woman—a teacher! Even today I cringe when I remember sixth grade and Ms. Horne."

Most teachers have to deal with infatuation, at least until like me they age into resembling pears bigger in the bottom than in the chest and with legs so thin and hairless they are almost invisible. Decades ago when the sweet bird of youth still perched on my collarbone and fluffed her feathers alluringly, a student came to my office every day at eleven o'clock and cried, between sobs mumbling about love and looking doe-eyed and carnally needy. Eventually I hid. I put a chair in the men's lavatory and at five minutes before eleven I retreated to the bathroom. Occasionally I peeked out. The course of infatuation usually runs shallow, and by twenty minutes after eleven the girl had vanished from the hall outside my office. After missing me for eight days, the girl stopped coming to my office. Of course my becoming an habitué of the men's john probably raised an eyebrow or two, not something to worry about, however.

Once when I lived in an apartment, a student parked her car beneath my bedroom window and for two nights slept in her car. I thought about cooking breakfast for her, but discretion mastered appetite. "How strange to meet you here," a student once said atop Primrose Hill in London. "Coincidence never ceases to startle," I said, though I had noticed the girl's following me ever since Gower Street. Today the morphing of *infatuation* into *stalking* has transformed the harmless, and, occasionally, the flattering, into the dangerous. In any case treat lovelorn children kindly but firmly, keeping them at arm's length. In arguing that children's books should delight as well as instruct, John Locke said that children had limited attention spans. Locke was right. In a day or two, something or someone more youthful and comely than you will likely attract their energy.

Reading

Sometimes I think books are and have been my life. For other people books are just one among many possible diversions. Encourage students to read. Justify your encouragement by letting them see your enjoyment, not by philosophy, sweeping statements that stray so far from ruler and chalk that they exceed the limited grasp of children. In general you should avoid the grand conclusion. This fall I received a telephone call from a woman writing an article for the *New York Times*. She had surfed postal codes on Amazon.com in order to discover what books were popular in different areas of the state. "My idea," she said, "is you are what you read." "No," I responded, "the opposite is true. People are not what they read about, but instead are what they do not read about. The painfully ordinary read books about celebrities. Rational cowards read about dead heroes. Walking corpses read books about the robust; dumbbells, about intelligence, and the poor about wealth. Meatballs read about people skinnier than pencils, and the deprived whose intimate lives are more conventional than grape Jell-O purchase books that describe gallivanters partial to caviar and kinky desserts with foreign names." "Goodness," the woman exclaimed, "you must have researched the subject." "Yes," I said. "You are fortunate to have talked to me. Otherwise you would have embarrassed yourself intellectually." Some time ago I received a letter from a policeman in Tennessee. The man had finished an autobiography and he wanted me to look at the letter he planned to send publishers along with the manuscript. "I joined the Highway Patrol," the first sentence read, "to help God in his fight against Satan." "Jesus," I thought, "I'd hate for this man to pull me over for speeding." Even worse, how would he react to my disobeying a roadside commandment and running a stop sign?

Thank goodness I have written myself into almost believing that within failure lurks the stuff of success, the essayist's version of the learning experience. Explanation is usually inadequate. Often we accept those explanations that sound or appear good in order to justify our own thoughts. This book will fail because I qualify what I say. Teaching has made me an examiner, a doubter, a prodder, and a questioner. Yet, despite what I write, I don't live as a questioner. I live a life rigorous with answers. I have, for example, never been to a casino, and I will never go to one because I think gambling destructively evil. The hard order that structures my daily life, though, becomes soft on the page, and I twist ideas until I wring qualifying, and occasionally enervating, thoughts from them. Even a fondness for reading, my favorite activity, can, I think, sometimes harm.

Many years ago an editor of an educational journal asked me to write an essay on "What and why you read to your children." At the time I had read my babies a library of books. For a long time I pondered a response. In part I read because I liked stories. Also, I was conventional and could rarely think of anything besides reading to do with the children. Since I had a bad back I could not play sports with them. And, of course, I read to keep the children from fighting. When I read they didn't quarrel, and the house was peaceful. Lastly, because Vicki and I did not go out at night, evenings were always free. Because I knew I would say foolish things that I'd later regret, I always refused invitations to dinner. A word could turn conversation unpredictable and disturbing, even frightening. In contrast the rigid page and shaped tale were relaxing and consoling to me. A book provides not only the illusion of ordering chaos but actual order itself. With attention focused on the printed word, I had both conversation and thought under control.

Truth is often too mundane for an article. I knew the editor wanted an instructive and inspirational essay. Behind her request lay the assumption that reading to children was educationally and probably spiritually beneficial, an assumption I wanted to be based on something other than hope. In my house George the dog is the only purebred. Vicki and I are mongrels. Yet like many parents we wanted American Education Club–certified offspring. We imagined our children being smarter and better than we are. Still, whatever effects reading has, if it has effects, are mysterious and vary from person to person. A mulch of books will not produce seedless blackberries or gifted children. If one of the goals of education is to rear better, sweeter people, grafting the enjoyment of reading onto a child may weaken rather than strengthen the stock. Books are fun, so much so that they can be opiates. For me love of people is more important than love of books. Could reading someday, I wondered, appeal to my children more than people? Many times I had fled from life to books. When the children grew up, I wanted people as well as books to fill their arms. I did not want reading to push good deeds and charity out of their everyday lives. Unable to justify my reading to the children in ways that would convert or inspire readers, I didn't write the article.

"Read not to contradict and confute," Francis Bacon wrote, "nor to believe and take for granted; nor to find talk and discourse; but to weigh and consider. Some books are to be tasted, others to be swallowed, and some few to be chewed and digested." Use the ideas I raise to help you consider. Munch a paragraph or two occasionally. What you don't like spit out. Just be careful that you don't spit them atop a new grave. If you do, they are liable to root and flourish. Once you have finished this book, read something else. Although reading can inhibit understanding by determining how a person interprets what he sees, more often than not it contributes to knowledge and enjoyment. Three years ago in Nova Scotia on a lonely lane I watched a large dragonfly eat a small dragonfly. I jotted down descriptions of the dragonflies in a notebook. I estimated the length of the large dragonfly at three and a half inches. The insect's eyes were green.

Bands of yellow wrapped its thorax while a chain of yellow tacks stretched, linked, atop its abdomen, the sharp end of each tack almost balanced on the flat head of the next tack. Red triangles adorned the top of the smaller dragonfly's abdomen while from the basal quarter of its hind wings saddlebags swung out reddish, dusted with brown. Although I searched the university library, I wasn't able to identify the dragonflies until the publication this past summer of *A Field Guide to the Dragonflies and Damselflies of Massachusetts*. Despite my notes the insects had remained scribblings. The book, though, transformed them into the lively stuff almost of myth, and my stroll along the lane into an adventure. I saw that the larger insect was a clubtail, the ferocious dragonhunter, while the smaller was a calico pennant, both insects habitués of streams and the boggy edges of woods.

You will, of course, run across many students who do not enjoy reading. Be enthusiastic about reading and encourage these students, but don't flay yourself if they do not leap into books shrieking with delight. Many of the most successful people I know are not great readers, and often what few books they read are junk. Still, junk like "great" literature diverts and can be instructive. Nevertheless, try to lure the uninterested into story. This fall a student wrote an essay for my class in which he recalled his early reading. If reading was a one-way ticket out of boredom, he asked, "Why doesn't everyone hop on the bus?" Unfortunately, he wrote, answering his own question, many young children first experience books as work, things heavy, assignments to be lifted and carried. "Kids," my student explained, "don't want to have to do something." Moreover, books assigned in schools were generally "awful." "I don't recall being given anything interesting to read until sixth grade when the teacher handed me *The Rats of NIMH.*"

For every "fun" book assigned, the boy recounted, he had read four or five so dull that "I can scarcely recall a single title." "Read it; it's really good," teachers said, then handed students *The House on Mango Street.* "I'm well read enough now," the boy wrote, "to recognize achievement in writing, but in the eighth grade the story of a young Hispanic girl's coming of age bored me to tears. *The House on Mango Street* is the type of book that can be appreciated only after a person likes reading. However, teachers think it concise, simple, and elegant, ripe with diversity and imagery. Just the thing," the boy stated bitterly, "for millions of eighth-graders to plod through." Too often, he then said, teachers ignored the one criterion that matters: "Will kids want to read this?" "Whenever I meet someone who dislikes reading," the boy concluded, "I always say, 'You just haven't found a good book.'" The boy's reaction to assignments is not typical. He is now the sort of person who reads everything, *Prevention* magazine if he finds it on a table, old newspapers used for packing in the attic, and shelves of books, good and terrible. What the boy said, though, is partly true. Many students need to be lured to reading, not pushed. For such students the bait may lie beyond a conventional reading list. If you fail to make readers out of such students, however, don't worry unduly. You cannot always succeed. You have many other responsibilities. In any case, years often bring great intellectual changes. Sometimes yesterday's nonreader is today's bookworm.

Math

I am a counter. I count the slices of pepperoni on a pizza, the steps from the front door of my house to my office in the English Department, and the number of times a day I hear students use the word *like*. I started writing this book two weeks ago. In fourteen days I have written 45,861 words, for an average of 3,275.8 words a day. During one of the fourteen days I didn't write, and on two others, classes exhausted me and I wrote little. In 1994 I spent two weeks cruising on Cunard's *Crown Monarch*. Because I lectured on writing memoirs, Vicki and I received free cruises, saving $3,470. Although the trip was complementary, I doled out $700 for gratuities and "port and handling charges." Next door to us, the children shared a three-person cabin. For each child I paid $1,940, or a total of $5,820. During the cruise additional charges amounted $1,483, of which $1,367 was for tours taken when the *Crown Monarch* visited a port. Of the remaining $116 of costs, $66 was for laundry, almost all the rest being for soft drinks the children drank by the pool. I did not drink anything alcoholic during the trip. For her part Vicki had only two drinks, the first a sunset-colored mango concoction when we sailed. She drank the second, a brandy Alexander, during a discussion of how our trip had become the children's trip. For the two weeks, I paid $8,003. On the voyage I gave three forty-five-minute lectures, each lecture, I figured, costing me $2,667.67 or, if calculated on the basis of minutes, $59.28 a minute.

Robert Frost once said that poetry was "a momentary stay against the confusion of the world." Alas, many people's stay against confusion and their own mortality seems to be anger. Unfortunately I don't think even a high-powered regimen of poetry would palliate that anger. Literature is not a pharmaceutical and won't cure the ills of life or society. Of course schools often prescribe books to children in hopes of shaping better people. Schools build reading lists around books that celebrate kindness and illustrate that different people are just people, not bad or evil, only different. The idea behind prescribing books is decent. If what we read determines how we think and act, then childhood reading can shape not only children but the future. The rub is that society prescribes books only for children. If people really believed that reading cured ills, then ethicists would prescribe books: for mature daughters mistreating an aged parent, *King Lear;* for the adulteress, *Madame Bovary;* for the father neglecting a daughter, *Dombey and Son;* for the son threatening to drop out of school and join the army, the poems of Wilfred Owen and Siegfried Sassoon.

Claims made for the effects of math are usually not as exaggerated as those made for literature, probably because higher levels of math are not as accessible to the general public as are books dubbed "higher reading." The claim most frequently heard is that "math trains the mind." If one grants that activity trains the mind, the statement is true but so broadly true as to be meaningless. If math trains the mind, so does splitting wood, grooming a dog, jogging, scrubbing floors—anything and everything. The useful old statement that discipline is genius does not mean that discipline can transform a person into a genius. Instead it implies that hard work leads to accomplishment.

To my mind math is one of many languages that is nice to know. As not everyone can be a good writer, not everyone can learn math. Most people cannot read a landscape. They cannot read history from a stone wall. They cannot read boards. They cannot scan an abandoned pasture. Stands of field birch and autumn olive tell them nothing about the pasture. They might as well be looking at Urdu. Not to know math, as not knowing books or one's backyard, diminishes existence, but not fatally so. The emphasis placed upon math by the SATs is wildly inflated. Enable your students who like math to progress rapidly. Don't hold them back and undermine their enthusiasm by confining them to classes full of students who dislike math and have little aptitude for it.

Instead help this second group of students discover subjects they really enjoy. In part my son Edward chose Middlebury College over Duke because at Middlebury he did not have to take math courses. "Why should I spend my college years studying subjects that don't appeal to me?" he said. "I love English and art history. I want to take more Latin and learn a spoken language. I'm eager to explore philosophy and archaeology."

Unlike Edward I "loved" math in secondary school. I took a math test every day for four years in high school. As a result

I'm comfortable with numbers, and I enjoy playing with them. Also, at least six times a year, I suffer from a recurring nightmare. I am walking to math class and I have not prepared for the day's test. Never do I take the test, however, because I always wake up sweating. Do your best to make your students comfortable with numbers. Rote learning is important. Make students memorize the multiplication tables. Memorization makes numbers familiar. Once students memorize the tables, for example, they can solve problems easier and begin to play. Recognizing the process used to solve a problem is not enough. Solving problems builds confidence. If possible introduce play and delight into class. I spent hours on plane geometry, fashioning not the shortest proof but ornate, involved proofs. At higher levels math becomes almost like philosophy, not something that concerns most teachers.

Math may not train the mind, but for me it was good training for writing. Outlines for essays resemble geometry proofs. The clarity of simple math resembles the clarity of a declarative sentence. Suggest to students who are having trouble writing clearly that they think of composing an essay or term paper in terms of solving a math problem. If their sentences trail down the page and in and out of meaning, compare writing to math. Compare explaining thought to solving a problem. As each step in solving a problem is discrete, so each sentence in an essay should be clear and uncluttered. Math creates only the illusion of order, but that is also what successful writing does. Even writing that tries to convey chaos must create order if it is to be read.

"The study of the history of bees and ants would do people as much good as the study of human history," declared Frederick W. Robertson, a popular nineteenth-century Anglican minister. Instead of learning from history so that we do not repeat the past, history teaches that humans never learn and always repeat the past, no matter their knowledge. The lesson is discouraging and is too cynical for young students, maybe even for adults. In trying to approach truth, be careful not to extinguish hope. Many times my children asked me not to talk at the dinner table. "Your tales are always gloomy," Eliza said, "and I am too young for gloom. I want to believe that life can get better."

Never forget that you are not a student. Realize that you should not discuss much of life with your class. One evening in bed when I was feeling "perky," I rubbed my foot against one of Vicki's feet. "Sam," she said, "I don't want to be hovercrafted tonight." Husbands and wives who have bumped along through years together recognize Vicki's remark as emblematic of a good marriage, something a person long accustomed to and relaxed around her mate would say. Young people would misunderstand the remark, thinking it indicated separation and frustration rather than union and jovial, if not lusty, good humor. Teach the stories and motivations of history, but in doing so realize that your students haven't lived long enough not to misunderstand. Offer hope and, much as I hesitate to suggest it, draw morals, wrapping them in the cloaks of motivation and effect. Age teaches that moral hunting is an easy sport. Whenever people search for morals they find them. Once school days have ended or youth is over, success in living depends heavily upon suspending judgment and not reducing happenings to the moral, thus narrowing existence. You are teaching children, however, and your responsibility is social. Awaken thought and attempt to make students see the beauty of decency. Be aware, though, that emphasis upon morality can lead people into both evil and absurdity.

My influence upon the behavior of characters in my books like that upon my college students is minimal. Voluna Hardaker studied librarianship at David Lipscomb College in Nashville for a year. As a result when the new library opened at Cross Keys, Voluna was appointed librarian. Voluna was a member of the Church of the Chastening Rod and as a creationist she believed science undermined Christian living. At Cross Keys she catalogued books according to library morals, not library science. She scraped the Dewey decimals, saying evolution had corrupted the system. For the sake of the new generation, she told a friend, she shelved books according to the sex of authors, separating those written by women from those by men. "Just think what thoughts might rise in the head of one of our precious little angels if she saw a book written by a man pressed hard against one written by a woman."

I agree with Frederick Robertson. A person can learn as much about good living from a science course as from history. Would that schools taught more classes that focused on the environment. Such courses blend well with other classes: history, philosophy, sociology, and English, among others, in addition to biology and chemistry, all the hard and soft sciences. For years

I have taught a course on American nature writers. In part I began writing about nature in reaction to teaching. "How narrow I am," I thought one day after class. "I can twist words into love knots and make thought dance. I can blaze paths through worlds of books, yet I can't name the trees and wildflowers growing behind my house." Teaching did not teach me, but teaching broadened my life, something it will also do for you. Teaching awakens curiosity and thus points the way beyond gloom and ignorance.

Letter Ten: Last Thoughts

DEAR TEACHER,

Practical concerns will fill your hours. You will spend many days preparing students for tests demanded by state or national governments. The location of your school will determine test results more than will your teaching. You will probably resent devoting so much time to the tests, thinking, probably rightly, you could accomplish more if you did not have to focus on the tests. The tests are important, however, for students. Often such tests determine funding. If constant drilling enables a goodly number of students to pass tests, even if their skills soon slip away, more money may become available for your school. Indirectly, perhaps directly if more teachers are hired, the money may contribute to bettering learning. What students learn quite often are not subjects but how to take tests. They learn craftiness, something useful to be sure, but not necessarily enriching.

Francis was the first of my children to take the SAT IIs. He made an 800 on the English test, though he wasn't fond of English. The topic he wrote on was "The nail that sticks out gets hit on the head by the hammer." "Dad," he explained, "graders spend two minutes on an essay. To ace the test all a student has to do is use big words and furnish socially appropriate examples." I asked Francis what examples he cited. "I started with Martin

Luther King, Jr. then skipped to Jesus Christ. I was home free after those two, but for good measure I tossed in Galileo, Charlie Chaplin, and the French Revolution." "What?" Eliza said. "No woman? Not Marie Curie or Rosa Parks?"

Print reporters are fond of asking about television. "How has television influenced students?" one reporter asked me, expecting an answer explaining that television undermined literacy and morality. "Look," I said, "a hundred years from now people will long for the good old days when children watched television and stayed out of serious trouble. Besides," I continued, "television is more dangerous to adults than to children. How many children leave husbands and wives, hoping to tumble about in the fleshly pastures depicted on soap operas?" Most programs on television would bore the behind off an elephant. Aside from a rare show on natural history or an adaptation of a Victorian novel whacked together by the BBC, I watch almost nothing. Never have I watched an episode of a situation comedy. In class last semester I criticized television, saying no channel appealed to me: MTV, Food Network, Fox, Disney, ESPN, Cartoon, and MSNBC. "You'd think differently," a girl interrupted, "if there were an Old English Teacher channel."

Although television does not appeal much to me, I don't think it as harmful as the "commentariat" proclaims. Arguments used against watching television today are the same as those leveled against reading fairy tales in the eighteenth century and novels in the nineteenth. Critics said fairy tales inflamed the imagination and undermined diligence. They lowered the tone of the mind and induced indifference to "common pleasures and oc-cupations." They delineated human life "in false colors" and raised expectations that could never be realized. They appealed to the imagination rather than to understanding and lured people from the rugged road of a good life. Stories that described the trans-formation of "Beggars to-day" into "Lord to-morrow" and "Waiting maids in the morning" into "Duchesses at night" made people contemptuous of "humble and domestic duties." Like any-thing else, television can be abused and is abused. Think of televi-sion as one of the bells and whistles available to you. Instead of condemning television out of hand, turn it to your use. Pull it out of your toolbox occasionally and use it to construct a lesson.

Vicki's father was a fine teacher, and in graduate school I took two courses from him. The courses were seminars. He sat at one end of a table and students sat along the sides and at the other end. Sometimes when he was asked a thorny question, he paused and took a pipe from the front pocket of his coat. Studi-ously he broke the pipe apart and cleaned it. Then he removed a can of tobacco from the left side pocket of his jacket. Next he pinched tobacco from the can after which he tamped it down into the pipe. Then he pulled a packet of matches from his pocket, struck one, and lit the pipe, sucking in powerfully. Once the pipe was lit, he leaned back, puffed deeply, studied the ceiling for a moment before rolling forward and looking down the table, said, "Gentlemen, there are no easy answers."

As a footnote let me add that when I was in graduate school Vicki was a schoolgirl, and I did not know her. There has been some confusion about this matter. When *Dead Poets Society* appeared, the *Richmond Times-Dispatch* interviewed my cousin Sherry. Sherry reported that I had met Vicki while I was a student. Vicki was "thirteen when she first met Sam," Sherry said, and the paper reported it. The truth is that I did not meet Vicki until she was twenty-one. All my life I have been trustworthy around everything sweet except chocolate cake. In any case, although the reply of Vicki's father evoked gales of silent chuckling, the reply was right. For most matters answers aren't easy. When I attended elementary and high school, streaming and programs for gifted students didn't exist, at least not in Nashville. Among students in every class I took were boys, mostly boys who were much older, having failed grades repeatedly, probably suffering from what we now know as dyslexia. Classes were large, in elementary school forty or forty-two, and good students did not receive extra help. Having to take classes amid children of lesser intellectual abilities did not bother good students. Moreover the good students don't seem to have suffered academically because they were not pushed to the edge of their abilities. Memory is often sentimental, but I think we got along well together. We didn't feel deprived. We were just children among children, no matter the grades we made. Later, members of the class did well academically, some becoming scientists, professors, lawyers, and doctors.

Times have changed. Most schools divide students into streams based on abilities. The streams are not bound within banks, and with little difficulty children can splash from one stream to another. "To put a brilliant math student in a class with kids who can hardly add is cruel and unusual punishment," a father told me. Because first-year French was not streamed in high school and the class crawled, almost not moving, Edward dropped French after a year, complaining angrily that he had learned nothing. "To hold a gifted child back, and that is what you are doing if you force the child to study only at grade level, is to waste a mind," a mother told me. Whenever I hear such remarks I want to reply, "But these kids are only ten and twelve. Who knows what twenty or, for that matter, thirty will bring?" After her freshman year in high school, Eliza spent a summer at Exeter in New Hampshire. She took senior classes. "We sat around a table and talked about books," she reported. "Everybody was interested. No one hacked around, and I loved it." For me on this subject there are no easy answers. Sometimes, though, I think classes for gifted students affect teachers more than pupils. Instructors must derive pleasure from teaching more intensely and at a deeper level than usual.

I also have mixed thoughts about the emphasis on ethnicity. No one who grew up privileged in the South in the 1940s and '50s, as I did, should begrudge affirmative action for African-Americans. What many people find nettlesome, however, is the bureaucratic spread of protected groups. An old saying seems applicable. The wise will always have to spend much of their time undoing the follies of the good. Perhaps you should not ponder such matters but just teach children. Still, emphasis on and re-warding people for their ethnicity is divisive and potentially dangerous. For my friend Josh ethnicity is a hard vault. A picture of

Serbians near Sarajevo digging up their ancestors, he said, was "the emblem of our age." "No matter where the Serbs go," he said, "they carry with them a past rotten with ancient quarrel and corruption. If man looks at the world through the eye sockets of the dead, he will never see for himself. Ghosts will haunt his days and stand between him and decency. The man who worships bones worships evil."

You will learn that the effects of classes are unpredictable. Even classes taught with high intentions can have low results. Indeed because the goals of such classes are lofty and thus often vague, they are the classes most liable to cause you disappointment. Every spring local teachers assign units on the American Indian. Instead of making them admire Indians the units angered my children. "I am tired of Indians," Eliza once complained. "They are always too good. Why can't we read about some bad ones?" "I have studied Indians for six years," Francis said, "and I have never met a real Indian." "That's because you have never been to a casino," Eliza said. "Many people in Mansfield are Polish and Italian," Edward said. "Why don't we do projects about them?"

And yet you must be aware of difference. Life has a way of milking bad effects from good intentions. People so misuse the goods of this world that they become bads. The abuses of correctness are the stuff of anecdotal legend. Usually not so colorful as the bad, the good does not lend itself as readily to copy and paragraph. Never forget that teaching is a high duty, one, indeed, structured around many low activities but still high, and at its best noble. You must stand for the virtues that "correctness" has tried to promulgate: decency, compassion, kindness, toleration, and understanding. Make your classroom a place where all children are welcome. Insure as best you can that students do not let cultural, racial, and religious differences become the materials of hurtful humor and conversation. Absolute freedom of speech has no place in the good elementary or high school classroom. Virtue and learning, children themselves, thrive best in out-of-the-way, protected places.

In *Areopagitica,* John Milton wrote, "I cannot praise a fugitive and cloistered virtue unexercised and unbreathed, that never sallies out and sees her adversary, but slinks out of the race, where that immortal garland is to be run for, not without dust and heat." Milton's rich language is seductive. Sounds become sense, as in romance feeling often becomes thought. When applied to childhood education, Milton's statement is wrong and dangerous. Protect your students. Help them grow strong, so that when hard winds of prejudice and evil rage around them they don't break. If they are old enough to understand, explain ideals to them. Be yourself such a dreamer that they become people who want to better their small worlds. By tacking the word *political* to correctness, opponents have tried to stain learning and behaviors that implicitly criticize "things as they are." You are in the classroom to make things better than they are. If someone accuses you of being against free speech, boldly declare your opposition. Say that you support wholesome all-American speech. Not only are you teaching children; you are responsible for children. Teach them to read and write, to enjoy math and chemistry, and make your classroom a place luminous with decency. You must be strong enough to stand up for correctness, no matter the pejorative words attached to it.

Things will always go wrong in class. You will be disappointed. You will change assignments in hopes of teaching a subject or unit better. The unit will go worse. You will ask for advice. The advice will fail. You will read books. The books won't help you. One morning everything will go wonderfully well, and you won't be able to figure out why. Everything is fallible; the only infallible item I have ever read about was a mousetrap, rather instructions for a trap that was infallible. "Open mouth," the instructions read. "Place a hunk of cheese far back on the tongue. When whiskers of mouse tickle teeth, bite down swiftly."

When you become so accustomed to failure that you do not let it disrupt teaching and when you realize that you cannot solve all your students' problems, you are on the way to becoming a good teacher. Terrible things happen to students. Be kind and concerned enough to send them to counselors. Many problems are beyond your knowledge. If you try to solve them, not only may you harm students but you will wear yourself out and neglect other students in the class. After you send a student to a counselor, talk to the counselor. Counselors are often overworked, and occasionally students vanish into a workload.

Elementary and high schools function in part as support groups, supporting students, families, and faculty. "As soon as I entered the university and certainly the first day of it, my father died," a Syrian girl wrote in an autobiographical paragraph. "After that I became a girl hesitance in every thing. My mother becomes crazy, because we haven't money to live after death my father. Just then my uncle took the house we lived in. After some days later he comes to our shelter to take the furniture. Meanwhile I can't prevent him because he is a strong man. One evening he comes to and said to me he doesn't want me to study at the university, because I am a girl. He said, 'You should marry and, you should let the studying.' After that I said with crying I didn't marry, and I didn't leave the university. Just then he threw me with chair and went. And when my mother heard me crying she comes and asked me why I was crying, but I didn't say anything. After some months ago my mother died with ill in her heart. After that I decided to let the shelter in the village and go away from the people. In the evening I threw myself in the river, but my friend saw me from his room's window and save me. At last I decided to work in a factory and to continuo the studying at unevercity. And now I am living with sorrow and pain." After I read the paragraph and handed it back, the girl asked me what she should do. I said, "I don't know." Although you may pretend to be arrogant and at times will be dogmatic, teaching will keep you humble. As long as you teach, you will be aware of how little you know and how unqualified you are to heal heartbreak.

Does this mean that you should avoid advising students? Certainly not—but tread carefully, if not lightly, on issues other than the academic. One December Pharaoh Parkus preached at the Tabernacle of Love in Carthage. When Pharaoh asked folks "to step out with Jesus," whole congregations waltzed toward the altar. At the Tabernacle when Pharaoh called people who had been smoking and drinking and staying out at night to come forward, half the congregation stood. "Tell it, Reverend," Dora Ludnum hollered from the back of the church. "Preach it, Reverend. You're getting them." After Pharaoh asked men who had burning sinful thoughts about women and those women who had hot thoughts about men to come forward almost all the rest of the congregation rose. "That's right, Reverend," Dora shouted. "You just preach it." When Pharaoh called those "captives" stung by bad thoughts about boys to come to Christ, Mr. Billy Timmons left the organ and joined the horde at the altar. "That's right, Reverend. Amen," Dora shouted, sitting in her pew and waving her fan. "You done it at last. You done got them all." Pharaoh was silent for a moment. Then after eyeing Dora up and down, he said, "Now I wants to see you old sisters who been walking around this here church, full of snuff and gossiping." "Damn it, Reverend," Dora shouted. "You done stopped preaching and gone to meddling."

Teachers meddle and preach. I always end the last class before a weekend a little early. Be good boys and girls, I say, and you'll be happy. I warn students against drink. I tell them not to get into a car with people who have been drinking. I warn them against cigarettes and "dope fiends." I urge them to be kind and tolerant. I encourage them to think about people less fortunate than they are. I go on and on. As the students walk out of class they smile at me, some because I seem a fuddy-duddy but others because I seem to care about them. "Sometimes," I say, "I think of you as my children, and I want you to have good lives." For moments, for the semester, they are my children, and I wince, because of hope and fear.

Problems

Schools are society's tuning forks. When society vibrates, schools quiver. Teachers do not live in ivory towers. In comparison to teachers, bankers and brokers inhabit isolated worlds. Momentary concerns swirl through schools before they touch other social institutions. To some degree being part of momentary concern is invigorating. In part it is wearying. Teachers never escape sexual doings. Years ago when a man repeated a slogan, saying, "Would you let a homosexual teach your child?" I was ready. Instead of a flea in his ear I stuffed a hornet up his bottom. "A homosexual would be fine," I said, stepping toward him. "Heterosexuals are dangerous. Hitler and Stalin, and probably Judas, were heterosexuals. What would you think about Hitler teaching your child? You might like it, but I sure as hell wouldn't."

Don't respond as I did. I was an old teacher, and my fervor frightened the man. Of course, the ignoramus needed frightening. My doings aside, though, learn to turn matters around in your head, and then nod and say nothing. Many years ago in New York City a school board fired a superintendent, ostensibly because he insisted that elementary schools teach positive lessons about homosexual as well as heterosexual families. Shortly afterward, a woman from a foreign newspaper interviewed me. Did I, she asked, think schools ought to teach such lessons? "The homosexual family," I said, "is but one configuration of that larger entity, the alternative family. Here in Mansfield," I continued, "there are many alternative families. In that white house at the corner," I said, gesturing toward a window, "is a family consisting of two men, five women, and a clutch of children. I am not sure about the number of children. One of the women, as you might guess, is often heavy with child, so the number varies. Down the street is a very pleasant Episcopal family of three men, two women, and four children. Episcopalians don't breed so irresponsibly as other groups, and from what I understand the number of children in this family will not increase. On the other hand," I continued, "a Catholic family, consisting of six or seven women and a varying number of men, lives just across South Eagleville Road. Because all members of the family are orthodox and eschew birth control, the number of whelps is extraordinary. In spring they scamper across the highway like squirrels. Occasionally one is mushed and sent back to his maker but, no matter, he is soon replaced. Thus," I said in summary, "you can see that the number of configurations of alternative families is immense. To teach children about all the existing variations in just this small community would fill the academic year and probably rupture the educational system. Until the school year is expanded and July and August are strapped like trusses onto the calendar, perhaps teachers should, for the moment, concentrate their pedagogical energies on lesser matters, say, such things as reading and arithmetic."

The woman wrote an article, but since it was published in Spain I did not read it. Realize, however, that the concerns of newspapers will eventually touch your school. Often concerns are athletic, and nothing more than an assembly attended by athletes will disturb your day. Nevertheless when controversy occurs in society, people often drag in schools. Almost invariably they draw upon Locke's legacy and state that since schooling shapes adults, schools have a duty to promulgate, and here is the rub: whatever dogma the group believes is important. No matter the ostensible separation between church and state, you will not escape religious doings. Students will pray for you and tell you so. Thank them and say something like, "I need all the help I can get." Other students will be more intrusive. One morning years ago after class, a student addressed me, saying, "I saw you go into the liquor store Friday evening. God does not want you to go into liquor stores." Because I taught at a university, and not an elementary or high school, my answer was brisk. "What!" I exclaimed. "God told me to go into that liquor store."

Sometimes a student will not answer the questions on your examination, writing something like, "I pray, Samuel Pickering, that you will listen very carefully to your born-again friends. They've got the answer. This may not be your idea of a final exam, but I wrote what the spirit moved me to write. I've got life eternal guaranteed, and it's wonderful. Do you?" You can fail such students, but before doing so give them the chance to take makeup exams. You should also talk to a counselor. The student may have a history of similar behavior. Such students are nuisances and can absorb time and drain energy. Teaching takes energy, however. Being in the world and involved with people is exhausting, and exhilarating. How lucky you are to come home tired, and agitated, but not bored. Agitation may, of course, provoke a heart attack and send you, as P. G. Wodehouse put it, through the gate in the garden wall. Even that has a positive twist. No people I know want to linger so long on the stage that they become burdens to themselves and to others.

In laboring to become saints, people become intrusive, and sometimes they become beasts. Not even being raised on Methodist pie makes you immune from "moral" criticism. People who attack schooling for what it is not doing are indirectly testifying to the high regard in which education is held. Society sometimes appears to think that as a teacher you are a miracle worker and, as such, groups will demand that you become their disciple. With math and geography, health and social studies, music and art filling your backpack, dealing with society's momentary concerns may seem too much. Of course, it is too much. But wouldn't you rather be, at least some days, in the "thick of things"? Very few professions are so exhaustingly involved in the everyday.

When the weight gets heavy, see if humor lightens it. The last time, or maybe the time before last, that people became agitated over school prayer, I wrote an essay focusing on religion and society. What came out resembled the result of a lesson plan, something very different from what I had intended. My subject shrank to "Business Prayer." I began by stating that I was acquainted with few sinners aged six to twelve. Most sinners really didn't hit their stride until after their schooling ended, at about age twenty-five. If Congress really wanted to reform the nation they should, I advised, begin with adults, not children, and make morning prayer a compulsory part of the business rather than school day. Ideas came to me easily for a while, but then I started thinking of exceptions. Airlines would have to be exempted from the law. No sane person would board an early flight to Chicago or Atlanta if he saw the pilot and copilot praying in the cockpit. An exemption would also have to be granted to the medical profession. If not, surgery would have to be scheduled during afternoons, for being rolled into an operating room and seeing the surgeon on his knees would, at the least, be unnerving.

The more I wrote the less practical business prayer seemed. If prayer made honesty popular and honesty became everyone's policy, the economy would collapse. The legal profession would disappear. Banks would fold like leaves on a mimosa tree. At the end of each letter sent to prospective customers in which bundles of money were offered at "modest" rates of interest, a vice president would feel compelled to write, "Ignore the enclosed advertisement. It is not for you. It will only bring you ruin and unhappiness." No longer would universities behave like circus barkers pitching education as the cure for all of society's ills. Of course, once educators told the truth, most universities, I realized, would close and I would lose my job. Suddenly business prayer seemed dangerous, if not un-American, and I stopped writing, concluding that prayer belonged just where politicians said it did, in the schools with fat yellow pencils and big orange notebooks, as far as possible from adults and the world of buying and spending. After the piece appeared I waited by the mailbox with a wheelbarrow, ready to help the postman unload his truck. I did not receive a single letter.

My experience is instructive. No matter how bright the lights around you seem to be, you are probably standing in a shadow. Few people notice or care what you do. No matter what the turmoil of the moment is, your duty is to your class. Friends often tell parents that children keep them young. The truth is that your class won't keep you young. Instead, you will keep your students young. You will introduce them to new activities and thought. You can bring spring to their lives. You can make them smile. You can be an example. You can't shape their lives but you can point and encourage. If you do so, someday you can say to yourself, "I haven't wasted my life."

I don't know where this book will carry you—not far because words are flimsy. As I look back over these pages, I marvel at how superficial and fragmentary my knowledge seems to be. Writers gesture and stop and start and never quite get things right. There are no easy answers and no easy classrooms or lives. Still, I know that if I stood by you in your classroom you would teach me many things. The sun would smile, and I would be gloriously happy.